Advance Praise

When we met Mara Linaberger in 20̶1̶7̶, ̶i̶t̶ ̶w̶a̶s̶ ̶l̶i̶k̶e̶ ̶m̶e̶e̶t̶i̶n̶g̶ someone we already knew. At first we thought she must just be "one of those people" with a personality and energy that is very welcoming and open. But on deeper examination, we saw she is "one of us". By that, we mean, one of a handful on the planet who have passionately dedicated their lives to the total wellbeing of children. Mara was born with a mission — and that mission is to save the children. To save them from the mental, emotional and spiritual stress of being just another number, a statistic, expected to help earn "Blue Ribbon" status for their school.

For the past 33 years the Good Knight Child Empowerment Network has been supporting parents and children with the tools necessary to have a safer, healthier life while also giving them the space to grow and learn in order to live each individual's purpose. During this time we have created a legacy of child advocacy and support in an environment that is conducive to the expansion of the mind and overall wellness of the individual child.

As you read *The Micro-School Builder's Handbook*, you will see why we say "she is one of us". You are holding in your hands the key to your child's future. The key to more family time, fewer tears and agony over homework, and to increased self-esteem. The key to being no longer affected by the letter grades on a report card. This book, coupled with Mara's guidance, is your blueprint to a crafting a happier, safer and healthier future for both you and your child.

Many blessings on your journey to a brighter future!
Sir Edward Jagen and Lady Sophia Key West,
The Founder & Chief of Staff for The Good Knight Child Empowerment Network, Inc., a 501c3 non-profit
Authors of: *When Angels Dream - Book of the North: Diary of an Angel Knight, Volume 1*

Just a few weeks ago my three children and I were thrown into the chaos of the school shooting that occurred at Marjory Stoneman Douglas High School in Parkland, Florida. The day after the shooting, my 12 year old son faced a code red lockdown in his middle school, just a few miles from site of the shooting. Not knowing if it was a real threat or not, the drill created a level of fear in my son that I've never seen before. Now, my outgoing, honor roll son who's loved school since Pre-k has anxiety and an upset stomach every single day and my husband and I face the task of getting him up and out to school each day - wondering if we will see him again in the evening.

The fortunate thing for me is, I've started working on a plan to open a micro-school in the fall of 2018 in our community - for my children and kids like them. What I know is this… it took a tragedy in my own back yard to light a fire in me to get this school opened. I know that what my micro-school will offer will be a safe haven for many kids who can't face going to their public school because of the shooting. And their parents will get to go back to thinking normal school thoughts like, "did he remember to take his lunch?" Instead of jumping at the sound of every siren or school phone call.

I have been fortunate to have the 8 foundational blocks to work from as this book was being written. And my son has become an integral part of my planning process. My hope for you, dear reader, is that you take the steps outlined and put them in to action - without the need for a traumatic event to motivate you.

Good luck building your micro-school!

Elaine Prestigiacomo,
Author of: *So You Want to Be a Healer: A Guide to Intuitive Development for Sensitive Souls*

Every day, I teach kids who are hungry and thirsty for deep, intellectual engagement that inspires them to become the absolute best versions of themselves... because I have the opportunity to work in micro-schooling environments. And when I have 8 students in front of me, versus the 20 or 30 other teachers work with in traditional schools, amazing things happen!

The Micro-School Builder's Handbook is desperately needed now because it gives concerned adults a how-to guide for creating, building, and sustaining their own micro-schools. Mara's advice is timely, practical, and very much needed in today's chaotic school climate. Anyone who is interested in being a part of truly student-centered education needs to discover more about micro-schools. This book will help them to begin that journey.

Lindsey Nelson,
Micro-School Educator, and Founder of, *Opportunity Unlocked,* Math, Science and Engineering classes for curious kids

I first met Mara at the 2017 *Archangel Summit* for purpose driven entrepreneurs in my hometown of Toronto, Canada. She was on stage in front of 3000 people, sharing her vision for transforming education globally through the building micro-schools as part of her *Archangel Moonshot* presentation. Her talk was inspiring, and aligned so well with my work at *The Personal Greatness Project,* I had to introduce myself.

I routinely witness parent's concerns and heartache about their child's place in an education system that's fallen behind the needs of its students. While students everywhere are trying to figure out who they are and where they're heading, they're often shown how to fit into a box instead of how to realize their true potential and discover who they're capable of being while at school. It's a recipe for mediocrity, and as much as we'd like to hope the problem will take care of itself, it's become clear that if our children are going to get the kind of education and leg-up on life we so badly want for them, it's up to us to do something about it.

Having schools that support student's self-realization is a must. Having an education that prepares them not just to survive but thrive in a quickly changing world should be non-negotiable. At *The Personal Greatness Project*, we believe there's something great inside every single one of our students, and having them experience that for themselves is a game changer. Mara's *Micro-School Builder's Handbook* is important, its a necessary blueprint, which has fortunately arrived right on time, to guide parents who want to create a place for amazing learning to happen for their children!

I couldn't be more excited or proud to be partnering with her on the first ever *Superhero Summit* — a five day gathering, which will bring families together to experience *The Personal Greatness Project* and to craft personalized learning plans for themselves!

Cory Chadwick,
Founder of *The Personal Greatness Project,* www.personal-greatnessproject.com

THE MICRO-SCHOOL BUILDER'S HANDBOOK

Personalized Learning for Your Child,

and an Amazing Business for You

Mara Linaberger, Ed.D.

The Micro-School Builder's Handbook
Personalized Learning for Your Child and an Amazing Business for YOU!

© Mara Linaberger, 2018

ISBN: 9781731228260

Throughout this book I have shared stories about the many parents and students I have been honored to serve. However, to ensure their privacy and confidentiality, I have changed some of the names and some of the details of their experiences. All of the personal examples from my own life are unaltered.

Cover Design: Jennifer Stimson

Cover photo courtesy of: Nancy Cabay Parker

Cover design concept: Jesse Malhotra

Editing: Anna Paradox

For

*Sir Edward, Lady Sophia, Princess Michaela,
and all of the Angel-Knights.*

With deep gratitude for the inspiration and support
you each offered to help me bring this micro-school
building handbook to the planet.

12

Table of Contents

Introduction: What Is Your Legacy?   19

Chapter 1:
Who Am I to Lead YOU?   30

Chapter 2:
WHY Build a School as YOUR Business?   43

Chapter 3:
Building Block #1-Frame your WHY with a PLAN   60

Chapter 4:
Building Block #2 – Get Legalities Out of the Way!   69

Chapter 5:
Building Block #3 – What's YOUR Special Sauce?   84

Chapter 6:
Building Block #4 – Location, Location, Location   97

Chapter 7:
Building Block #5 – Show Me the Money!   108

Chapter 8:
Building Block #6 – David vs. Goliath   123

Chapter 9:
Building Block #7 – People, People, People   136

Chapter 10:
Building Block #8 – Ready, Set, GO!   151

Chapter 11:
Obstacles, Pitfalls, and Screw-Ups   161

Conclusion: Your School as Your Legacy   167

Acknowledgments   170

About the Author   172

About the Cover   174

Thank You!   176

Foreword

There once was a Renaissance thinker named Paul Goodman. Paul was at one time or another a poet, novelist, teacher, psychologist, urban planner, social philosopher, and education critic. Right around the same time that he was dying – at far too young an age – in 1973, I was just starting out as a 19-year-old teacher in an inner-city free school. Paul's writings had a huge influence on me, particularly a book called *Compulsory Miseducation.* The title gives you a pretty blunt clue as to his sentiments toward our nation's monolithic approach to educating the majority of our children.

Paul was a lifelong resident of New York City. He even went to college there. His proposal for making his city's schools places where all children thrive, instead of so many being swallowed up like a bunch of young Jonahs, was to place at least one school on every single block. To critics who said the idea was absurdly utopian, that the city could never afford it, Paul replied, "Nonsense."

Not every adult in the school has to be a trained professional, he said. A few, yes, but mostly they have to really care about children and understand how to relate to them on the right levels. The schools he imagined would serve as community centers, too. Parents would get involved, as well as others from the neighborhood. Education would be a cooperative effort and not everyone would have to be highly paid. It would cost far less than a conventional school.

Paul listed other advantages to going small. Children's individual talents and needs would come to the forefront and not get lost in the crowd. There would be no call for the endless regimentation and repetition that turns so many children off. Oh, and you wouldn't have to force them to go because school would be so exciting and engaging that they would have plenty of reasons of their own.

This was one of the first things I discovered at my little school – the kids wondered why we weren't open on Saturdays, too. Extended holidays drove them mad.

And so Paul Goodman's vision was one of the first things that came to mind when I first met Mara Linaberger and she shared her vision of micro-schools with me. I mean it just makes sense, for all the reasons Paul pointed out 50 years ago.

Paul remains a hero of mine to this day, but I will go so far as to say that Mara's vision is even more sensible. It's no wonder, because he was never a mother, and he only taught young adults. He didn't spend over twenty years working with students and teachers in the public schools, nor did he ever actually start his version of the ideal school.

In addition to being a Renaissance individual like Paul, Mara has done all of these things too, and so her ideas about teaching and learning, and helping children reach their fullest potential, are grounded in real experience – and lots of it. They are far more than just good ideas.

I, like Mara and Paul, never seem to stop thinking about how to fix our broken educational system. We know what a different society we would be if our schools truly supported the blossoming of each and every child. Imagine an entire generation of adults every one of whom grew up learning to think for themselves and discovering their unique reason for being on this earth. Just imagine.

Some believe the system is so broken it can't be fixed. Others say the answer is simply to expect more from the teachers and the students, to restructure the curriculum and the school day so that they work harder and longer. My thinking, and I have written extensively about this issue elsewhere, falls somewhere in between those two extremes. We will never fundamentally change the system we have because the vested interests that created it in the first place, and continue to shape it today, are too powerful and don't want it to change. And we can't get rid of it because our grossly inequitable economic system leaves too many families without other options. So God bless all the committed people who keep trying to make our schools good places for as many kids as possible. They are my heroes too.

For me, the solution is to keep expanding a parallel network of educational alternatives, and then to make them as accessible as possible to children of all backgrounds. Not just one type of school or learning center, but many, many different kinds because children are all so different one from another. What a child on a reservation in the Southwest needs, and how he or she learns best, is unlikely to be the same as a child from the South Bronx, or one from a small town in Minnesota.

Now you can see why I like Mara's mico-school model so much. It's eminently flexible and adaptable. It's less expensive and therefore more affordable. There are no cracks for children who may need special kinds of attention to fall through. And above all, she makes it all so doable.

May this wise and practical handbook find a wide audience, and like a dandelion may it cast seeds everywhere that sprout into new and better places for children to learn and grow.

Chris Mercogliano,
March 2018, Albany, New York

Author of: *In Defense of Childhood: Protecting Kids' Inner Wildness; How to Grow a School: Starting and Sustaining Schools that Work; Teaching the Restless: One School's Remarkable No-Ritalin Approach to Helping Children Learn and Succeed;* and *Making it Up as We Go Along: The Story of the Albany Free School*

Introduction

What Is Your Legacy?

Education is the most powerful weapon which you can
use to change the world.

- Nelson Mandela

Are you someone on a mission? Someone who feels a
deep urge to do something of lasting value? Someone
who wants to leave a legacy when you are gone? If
you've picked up this book then perhaps you are...

- a "mompreneur" with kids, whose dramas around
  school make you crazy and unproductive at times in
  your business
- a burned-out teacher with a vision around teaching
  kids the way THEY need and want, while having fun
  supporting them as individuals

- a professional who has always dreamt of working with kids but is afraid to go change jobs in order to go "into the trenches"
- a coach or mentor who works in teaching the spiritual arts to adults, and sees the critical need for similar learning options for children
- a successful entrepreneur or angel investor who wants to transform or disrupt the big system of education

If you have ever created a business of your own, you already know that creating something new from scratch can be a challenge. First there's coming up with a unique idea or vision to transform situations or people. Next there is locating or generating the revenue needed to put that idea into action. And then comes the enormous task of taking action.

In all of the massive excitement that comes around finally figuring out your true purpose and putting passions into words so that you can share them with others, there's a tremendous amount of positive energy generated. But inevitably that energy can begin to wane when you become aware of all the action steps you will need to take to make the dream a reality.

The vision can begin to sag when the fun of dreaming and planning are done and the real work of taking action begins. Let's face it, most of us prefer the fun to challenging, but what often derails us is the actual work that has to get done, especially if we haven't planned things out in a doable, bite-sized manner.

If you've picked up this book then you are probably curious about micro-schools and are considering opening one of your own. Building a micro-school, whether you rely upon an existing model, purchase a franchise, or dream up a new and innovative alternative, is a huge undertaking. Some of the big areas you will have to tackle are: visioning, reviewing state laws and regulations, raising and managing money, securing a location, specifying or designing a learning "curriculum," hiring staff, recruiting students, purchasing insurance, and tending to finance.

Those tasks can seem downright daunting if you don't know the jargon, the quickest routes through them, or the pitfalls to watch out for.

One of the biggest traps I've seen in the school-building process is getting trapped in the fun stuff. There are the long and interesting meetings over coffee, the talking and meditating about vision and mission, the creative aspects of making flyers and planning family awareness events, and speaking about the idea in public. Getting stuck in those initial planning activities, however, can lead to a failure to launch your idea.

Take, for instance, the story of clients I worked with in Virginia. I first learned about their interest in building a micro-school for kids in a local newsletter. Their vision for a mountaintop wisdom school had been informed by the ideas and teachings of a mystic and teacher they all had all known and been drawn to study with over the course of 20 or so years. I met up with them in person and began the task of working through their shared vision and mission, to bring the shared dream into form.

From the very start, they were some of the kindest, most generous and joyful people I've ever collaborated with! They invited me to support two initial brainstorming meetings where parents and children were invited to talk about building a school together. These events were fun for everyone.

Each gathering included hands-on activities such as wand making or fairy house building. And there were excellent discussions about school. Parents and kids were invited to talk about what traditional school is or was like for them, and then about what a dream school might look and feel like. These meetings always included incredible food, wine, and lots of community building. They were so much fun for everyone!

But then came the task of moving beyond the dream lists, beyond the vision board process, so to speak. We headed into weekly meetings to determine our next steps. We talked about the kids who had showed up and what they needed. We looked at the dream mountaintop area where everyone hoped the school would be built someday. We talked about non-profit vs. for-profit status, and about how we might find seed money to get the school launched.

Knowing how important collaboration is to the micro-school building process, I did some legwork to locate schools in the area, and a possible launch location and non-profit partner. I found both in a local community center, housed in a former elementary school. I met with the executive director and spoke with the board to share the vision. We were thrilled to gain support from the center in whatever ways we needed.

So we planned and held two events in that location to see what sorts of families might show up to participate. Again, these days were packed with fun for everyone – this time including explorations in digital music, participating in laughing yoga, making wands, and working with crystals and gemstones. We had fewer families show up in this new location, but they were families living close by, who might enroll their children in the school if it launched at that location.

Now that we knew we had a place we could begin with real students, an idea that had merit and followers, it was time to do the real foundational work. It was then that the energies began to wane and the team suggested that we take a break. I was sorry, to say the least. We'd found a non-profit partner who was willing to share space, and we had a handful of kids and parents excited to get going. We even had a retired school teacher who wanted to get back in to service working with kids in new ways!

What I learned from this experience is this:

NO AMOUNT OF WANTING, DREAMING ABOUT, OR VISIONING WILL BUILD A SCHOOL.

Building a micro-school requires action.

And this book is all about that, about taking the actions needed to launch a small school. A micro-school.

The term micro-school is relatively new. It refers to a new movement in alternative education to reinvent the one-room-schoolhouse. Classes are typically smaller and multi-aged. Classes may be taught directly, or students may use technology or inquiry methods to explore ideas. Tuition is usually lower than neighboring private schools. Micro-schools borrow most of their ideas from the very best in education, offering students a smaller, personalized pathway for learning.

In the coming chapters, you'll find the steps you'll need to take in order to craft a sound plan of action for building the micro-school of your child's dreams. Unlike many of the books out there about alternative education and small schools that describe the characteristics and impact of particular small schools, this book will actually outline the steps you will need to take, leading to a sound plan of action. From there, you'll have a map to follow, a blueprint for building the school of your dreams.

Let's be clear up front. Building a micro-school is a large and complex process. Starting a school is a lot like riding a rollercoaster. It will be scary and fun, it's amazing and daunting, all at the same time.

And if you've got kids at home, the challenges you will face can easily multiply. The highs will be high and the lows low. At times, it may seem like there's never a moment to take a break and breathe. And sometimes it may feel like it will never be YOUR time. Frustration may build. And you may find yourself thinking things such as:

Am I crazy for trying to start build a school?

Why did I ever think I could do this on my own?

Is it even possible to create a new school in this crazy educational climate?

I'm here to tell you that yes, it IS possible to build the school of your dreams. One that makes you excited to get out of the bed in the morning to be of service. One that can potentially help you to earn money in ways that feel more like play than work.

And most importantly, you can create a micro-school, one that serves the highest growth and development of your amazing kid while also serving your community at the same time. I can assure you that, if you take things one step at a time, it is possible build and run a micro-school, while also raising happy, healthy, and deeply connected kids.

Take my client Ellen as an example. She's an author, an empath and intuitive, a holistic healer, who is building her business around teaching others to embrace their empathic and intuitive skills. Ellen really hustles to make ends meet. Sometimes she's running yoga or reiki workshops for kids after school (with her kids in tow) and other times she's doing angelic readings for clients over the internet. Other times, she's developing group instructional programs for adults, either face to face or online.

Ellen is passionate and creative, always putting out offers to see what sort of service her former and potential new clients might like her to develop. And she's usually going in about three directions at the same time. This split focus, ironically, matches her responsibilities as a mother by the way!

Ellen has three amazing kiddos: Liam 11, Sophie 8, and Elsa 4. When Ellen began to work with me on her micro-school building plan, her oldest two kids were in traditional schools, while Elsa was just preparing for pre-school. Ellen's mornings began early at 7 a.m. when she was up to help Liam and Sophie get ready for the bus, and to help her husband head off to his job. Once everyone was out the door at 8:30, Ellen would wake up Miss Elsa.

Once Elsa was up and fed, Ellen was able to start her day as an entrepreneur. First, she tackled the email and Facebook messages while Elsa played with her toys. She checked her calendar to figure out which hours she needed to ask her mom to watch Elsa while working directly with clients.

Ellen has tried having Elsa around while she's serving clients online and the results have been mixed. Sometimes Elsa is occupied and happy, while other times she crawls up into Ellen's lap for attention. Depending on the client, this is either a welcome opportunity to remember to tend the inner child, or it's an annoyance and interruption to the flow of the coaching.

This constant hustling for clients, serving her family's needs first, and juggling scheduling has gotten Ellen frustrated at times. Her personal practice is strong enough that she knows it's all part of the journey, but she often wonders when it will get easier. When she'll have the time and energy to get her business focused, a steady sales process in place, and her courses full to capacity with happy and grateful, high-paying clients.

If you are anything like Ellen, then you know that all of the distractions in your daily life are detrimental to your passion to build a business. The distractions might range from small children like Ellen's, to ailing parents, to a full-time day job that is sucking the life out of you. And you, like Ellen, are most likely unwilling to sacrifice your family time or your children's happiness to make your business work for you. Perhaps you even harbor subtle feelings of guilt, remorse, or shame for even wanting something more for yourself while raising a family.

It makes sense. Children are precious. They need us and, while they are young, we are responsible for them. And if you are in a marriage or relationship, your partner is important to the big equation as well.

But what is the real cost in not building the business of your dreams? What is to be gained in sacrificing yourself and your dreams for everyone else? What are you actually stating with your actions to your family? What are you teaching your kids that a strong and loving parent is and does?

Are you willing to pass on a misguided idea that women are here to serve everyone but themselves? Are you willing to teach your kids that sacrifice is more important than personal growth and fulfillment? Would you want your kids to grow up living their lives that way?

I'd like you to consider for just a moment that having it all is truly possible. That you can have the business of your dreams while also enjoying lots of meaningful time with your family, partner, or loved ones. And that those things can actually be combined to make life simpler for everyone!

Does it sound too good to be true? Well, this book is all about helping you to see that it's possible. That you actually can combine your dreams of a business along with taking good care of those you love – and make a huge difference in the world for others at the same time – by building a school to serve your kids and/or other kids in your neighborhood.

I have a vision for Ellen, and it's the same vision I have for you. Each morning, your alarm clock goes off and you rise to greet your children already up and getting ready for school. They are motivated, preparing themselves for the day because of excitement about the learning and activities that lie ahead. And you are able to get yourself dressed and ready for the day without even so much as a whine and whimper from your kids.

Whether you accompany your child to the amazing school you've built or not, your heart rests easy knowing that your child is engaged in rich learning and is loving the process all day every day. Even if you know you will just create the school and lead it, versus teaching in it, isn't the image amazing?

But then ... as so often happens, the bubble pops. The dream disappears. You find yourself back in the same old life.

Worrying that the bills won't get paid.

Worrying that your kids are being ruined by technology, by other kids, or by teachers and school.

Worrying that your kid will do something terrible at her current school because of all the stress and anger she's carrying.

Worrying about your child's safety with all of the bomb threats and school shooting events in the news.

Worrying that your spouse or partner is going to walk out because of all of the challenges you bear together.

Worrying that the planet is going to implode with all of us on it.

Facing your fears and tackling them is a big part of the work we are going to do together. We're going to take a long hard look at them, name them, and then dismiss them. Because awareness is the first step in changing anything I'd love to ask you to stop for a few minutes and get a blank sheet of paper. Take a few minutes to write down all of the fears you have about yourself, your business, education today, and your kids and your spouse/partner (or your support systems if you are single).

Create big categories and then write out all the things that worry you. Now put that list aside. We will come back to it as we dig in to the process of creating the business you love!

Let's get going. This book is designed to show you the way.

What lies in store...

In the coming chapters I'll share a simple 8-step process you can use to lay out the school of your dreams. It will not only be the school that helps your child to love learning again, it will become a part of your community, and make a difference for many other kids. And that's all in addition to creating an income for you, if you choose to go the route of creating it as a for-profit business. How awesome is that?

Chapter 1

Who Am I to Lead YOU?

I will not be the first to seek a vision of education
that brings together the need for
wide-awakness with the hunger for community,
the desire to know with the wish to understand,
the desire to feel with the passion to see.

- Maxine Greene

Maxine Greene's words have inspired me to create new learning opportunities for kids for some time. Perhaps her words have touched your heart as well and you are ready to create a place where your child can truly pursue his passions all day, every day.

Before we get rolling on the planning, you may be wondering who am I? And what authority do I have to give you the free license to start your own school, to take back education for your child, and the children of the future? Allow me to share a bit about myself and my story.

Born, raised, and still living in Pittsburgh, PA, USA, I'm an author, artist, musician, and mindful technologist. But first and foremost, I'm a life-long learner and professional educator.

In my "first life," I had a career in traditional education that spanned over 20 years and included teaching in an inner-city, arts-focused magnet school. My work then morphed into several years of coaching and doing teacher professional development full-time, and serving as a district administrator in my final formal position.

After downsizing eliminated my school district position, I decided to create my own educational technology consulting business. I've served small business owners, and have collaborated with larger businesses and colleges. I have also written groundbreaking online coursework for teachers around inquiry learning, digital portfolio creation, and creating more mindful classrooms.

Having published my first book, *HELP! My Child Hates School: An Awakened Parent's Guide to Action*, I now specialize in the creation of micro-schools to meet the differing needs of today's kids. My first book was aimed at helping me to identify kids and families who are in crisis, no longer able to function within the traditional school model. The steps I outlined helped guide parents to the best educational settings for their kids. And one of the options I shared in my first book is to create a school of your own.

Over the past four years, I have worked with several different groups around the notion of creating a modern, technology-infused one-room-schoolhouse. My vision was that some kids would be better served in a small, multi-aged, independent, and individualized learning setting where they would be known and valued by everyone. I imagined technology being utilized to support each child's curiosity, connecting them to other children as well as top experts around the globe. And I was excited to see if I could make this vision into a reality.

My first attempt at building a micro-school came in talking with some visionaries in my hometown of Pittsburgh, PA. These professional friends listened critically as I worked out my jumble of ideas, culling through 20 years of traditional education experience, to come up with *a simpler model and a plan for school creation that could be put in to action.* We held several meetings in a small post-industrial steel town on the Ohio river before the momentum waned and I took a step back to regroup.

I have learned a lot about micro-school building through collaborating on the process with families. You'll find these lessons sprinkled throughout the book.

Lesson Learned: Parent interest, commitment, and buy-in are a primary key to success in building a school. Without them, there is no purpose to the building process.

Without children of my own, as a micro-school builder, I rely on the interest of parents and kids to get the ball rolling in building a school. Otherwise, I would need to function like Kevin Costner's farmer character in *Field of Dreams* – building the micro-school so that the students could come.

In the case of my first school building group, the two families I connected with were definitely interested in the small school concept and came to the meetings I scheduled. But their children were doing okay in school. During our initial planning phases, one family actually transferred their kids into a new public charter school. It became apparent to me that without a crisis of some sort, without a real need on the child's part, action on the parents' part would not happen. Without the urgent need for something different for their children – or for themselves professionally – these parents' motivation to work on building a new school for their kids and themselves just wasn't a top priority.

Lesson Learned: Unless there is some sort of educational crisis or specific need not being met on the part of a child, many parents will leave their child in the big system of school.

Around this same time, I began to investigate the legal options for opening a school in Pennsylvania. I found that the two most common methods for opening a school are to apply for a charter school license from the state department of education, in cooperation with the local school district where the charter school will operate. The second is to apply for a private school license from the state.

I paid a visit to the state department of education in my home state of Pennsylvania to investigate the process of opening a private school. After the four-hour meeting, I was handed a large stack of paperwork to be completed in addition to preparing for a site visit from officials from the department of education. In a nutshell, in Pennsylvania a private school applicant must have everything in place, the school staffed, and students enrolled, before the state representative will visit to grant licensure.

The process for gaining a public school charter license was no less daunting either, requiring a similar level of preparation and a presentation to the local school board to be granted licensure. Interestingly, in most cases in Pennsylvania, a charter school application is rejected the first time it is shared at the school board level, and requires working with the state department of education to gain approval. I couldn't see how all of this effort would help my vision of making learning more organic, lighter, and fun for everyone involved.

And so I went back to the drawing board, convinced that there had to be another way.

My next adventure in micro-school building was with parents in another small river town, this time in the Blue Ridge mountains of Virginia. Again, I befriended two moms of unique kids and began a dialogue about what wasn't working in school and what we might do about it. And again, the issue of time, commitment, and buy-in came to the forefront. We met in a local coffee shop, talked alternative learning, and even envisioned utilizing space in a local art cooperative non-profit. Both of these moms had full-time jobs, and so they weren't quite ready to go all in on the process of creating a school for their children. In the end, one of the two moms ended up pulling her daughter out of school and enrolling her in a cyber program so that she could learn from home. The school building project ended there.

Lesson Learned: If a parent is just concerned with their own child's needs, or if the situation is too severe for the child, parents often turn to home-schooling or cyber schooling as a quick fix. This often negates the need to build a micro-school, at least early on.

It was during this time that I also began to look for existing or emerging alternatives to setting up as a formally recognized school. I wondered if others were tackling the same basic issues of public charter schools and private schools.

I located a group called North Star, who had created a new option called the "Liberated Learner's Network." Supporting parents of middle and high school students who had neither the time, energy, or interest in home-schooling their kids, the network took over the parental role for these kids. With the group acting as more of a mentor space and learning center, students are signed out as homeschoolers but supported in their learning plans by the staff at the center. North Star is in the process of expanding its network and offers paid webinars to allow parents to consider opening a center for their child in their own hometown.

While the model made sense to me, the urge to build something slightly different persisted in my mind and heart. I can see the ease of choosing to open a franchise school, and the usefulness of being part of a network. But the notion of creating a method for people who want to build their own unique school, that could be used to work quickly and efficiently through the processes, kept speaking to me.

Upon my return from Virginia, I decided to take a break from talking with families about building schools to do some deeper research. I settled on examining currently existing one-room schoolhouses more closely to determine best practices and processes they had in place to help them flourish.

I read about some new schools as well as about several different hold-outs, small schools built long ago in remote places which had maintained enrollment and continued to function. I located some examples of one-room schoolhouses in the ski valleys of Colorado as well as on a group of small islands off of the coast of Maine. I decided, as it was the end of summer, a visit to the schools in Maine would be fun.

I'd read about six island schools in a book called *Island Schoolhouse: One Room for All* by former one-room teacher Eva Murray. Matinicus Island sounded like a good starting place for my research and I understood that Eva was still living on the island. So I reached out directly and Eva connected me to the island's superintendent to schedule a visit.

Imagine my surprise when Eva also shared that the school board was having difficulty locating a teacher to open the school at the last minute to accommodate three new students on the island. One thing led to another. I talked with the superintendent via Skype and he encouraged me to come up to visit and to interview for the open teaching position.

I'll be honest, I had my misgivings. It had been nearly ten years since I had been in an elementary classroom. Not only that, I sensed that my real purpose for visiting was to gather information about the school. Intuitively I sensed that I could help get the school open and running, but that I lacked the stamina or temperament for teaching on a two-mile by one-mile island, twenty-three miles off the coast of Maine! I knew I'd be homesick.

The visit was incredible – I loved the island and the people. I was offered, and I did wind up taking, that job. I hurried home, gathered up the supplies I thought I'd need for 10 months on an island, and got the school opened and running a week later. But my intuition proved accurate. I did end up only staying through Thanksgiving because of the remote location.

The three months on the island, teaching in the one-room schoolhouse, was an adventure for sure. Not one I'll ever forget. The stories I can tell about living in such a remote place and running a one-room schoolhouse are fantastic, almost too unusual to believe.

The lessons I learned about myself and about a running small school, however, were profound and useful to share with you.

Lesson Learned: Small schools aren't the best environment for everyone.

On Matinicus Island, I learned first-hand that when a child has specific learning or developmental needs, the adults who serve that child need to have the training, skill sets, and temperaments for that work. That will be something to keep in mind as you think about your student population. Some children need more support than a small school can provide.

I also learned that I crave and need the support of other adults. In an isolated setting everyone knows everyone. As the sole educator I had no colleagues to turn to directly for brainstorming and support. At the end of the day I was on my own, with no social circles or establishments where I could let off steam from the stress of the day. So long as your school is within driving distance of a town or city, you'll be able to engage in the down time activities you need to keep your mind and heart strong and clear. Running a one-room schoolhouse requires lots of attention and energy – therefore, equal amounts of self-care are needed too.

Lesson Learned: Location and student population matter.

In the case of living and teaching on an island, isolation works great for some, and not as well for others. Children who attend any sort of small school will learn behaviors and habits from those around them. If there isn't enough diversity in age, temperament, or skill-set, kids may wind up learning more of what not to do than what to do.

Lesson Learned: A small school can't be run by one person alone.

Working on the island, I also realized that parent support and community support are critical. One person cannot effectively run a school in isolation, and all of the key players must be on the same page in order for the school to run smoothly. These are the kinds of things you'll need to tackle, and which I'll help you think through as we move through the process of framing your idea for a micro-school.

Coming back home to Pennsylvania from Maine, I felt a bit lost for some time. I still wanted to work on launching a micro-school but didn't know which way to turn next. I found myself going back and forth to Massachusetts, spending time with friends who were working at a retreat center. For a while, I had some thoughts that this location might prove fruitful for micro-school building, and again, I found interest but not an urgent need or commitment to making the micro-school dream a reality.

At this point, it became apparent to me that the single common denominator in all my starts and stops in building micro-schools was me.

I took some time to deeply meditate about my small school vision and realized I needed to do some practical learning, to actually get a handle on the big ideas and activities that would need to be accomplished in order to build a school from scratch.

I had attended a conference in Massachusetts while I was teaching on Matinicus Island, offered by the Alternative Education Resource Organization (AERO). Dedicated to providing opportunities for alternative school builders to gather, talk, share, and collaborate, AERO proved a great source of information! I signed up for AERO's "Start a School" online course. Even without school-building partners, I was determined to go ahead and build a school, sensing it was finally time to actually do the thing I'd so long dreamt about.

About a week after I started the course, I received an email from a group in the Charlottesville, Virginia area. I had attended several of their gatherings while I had been living there. The note described a separate group of adults who were holding meetings to discuss the creation of a small school for children. I immediately wrote to the three leaders mentioned in the email: a well-known author, the president of a spiritual study group, and the woman who had the vision for the school.

After a few brief phone calls, I realized I'd met folks who felt very much like "brothers and sisters from other mothers." And so I invited three of the key players to join me in the online school-building course. Over the next six months or so, we completed the course and framed out the group's vision for a small "Wisdom School" in the Afton Mountain, Virginia area. We convened several workshop days to see who might be interested in our school ideas. While attendance was low, those parents and kids who did show up were of the sort that fit the model we were beginning to frame up.

As I mentioned in the introduction, we began to lose steam on the tasks in such a large undertaking. It was especially clear that the time wasn't right when we realized that only one of our team members was actually living in the community where we hoped to build the school. After some honest and difficult conversations, we decided it was best to pause our work together while each member tended to the particular priorities in their lives.

During this same time frame, I began to write my first book *HELP! My Child Hates School: An Awakened Parent's Guide to Action*. It described the "new kids" and the ways in which school may not fit their interests, passions, and needs. I crafted it as part catharsis, to offer the wisdom I had hoped my parents would have been given, as well as a guide for parents to actually do something proactive when their child says they hate school.

In the book, I walked the reader through my thoughts and research into why school is the way it is, what it's designed to do, and why we might want to create alternatives. I offered lots of ideas about how to take progressive steps forward as a parent, advocating for the child with teachers and principals, getting to know your child's learning preferences and patterns, making changes quickly and effectively when needed. I also shared background information on the myriad of options available to parents today to make switching schools a breeze.

The book was published digitally in April of 2017, was picked up by a New York publisher in June, and will be available in bookstores on May 1, 2018.

Around the time I was finishing the manuscript for my first book, I was introduced to the chief of staff of a non-profit organization in Beltsville, Maryland, by my book mentor and coach, Angela. Sophia, the chief of staff at the Good Knight Child Empowerment Network was in charge of running a summer camp for kids in Good Knight Castle, in driving distance from both Washington, DC and Baltimore, MD. Successfully helping kids find their path while enjoying true freedom to learn independently, the Castle's summer camp had been a summer haven to Angela's son Jesse for six years.

Over the course of the next several months, while visiting the castle site and summer camp, Sophia and I came upon the idea of turning the property and existing programming into a year-round learning center for today's creative and independent kids. I'd finally found the school-building partnership I'd been searching for!

By the end of the summer of 2017, we'd set the foundation for the first micro-school in Beltsville, to be named "The Legacy School." I then found myself on the stage at an entrepreneurial conference, vying for a $50,000 "Moonshot" award. During my two-minute presentation, I talked about today's creative, quirky, motivated, and often entrepreneurial kids, who seem to be on a mission, even at their young age. I talked about my own mission: to create a network of 100 micro-schools for those kids in the next 20 years. And to convene a Superhero Summit where these same kids could meet in person to think, dream, plan, and share. While I didn't win the top prize at the Archangel Summit, I made lots of amazing connections and solidified my conviction to write *The Micro-school Builder's Handbook* as part of my 100 micro-schools mission.

Now you know a bit more about me and my varied experiences with micro-school building. Honestly, I've learned much more from my failures than from my successes. Should you choose to launch your own micro-school as an outcome to reading this book, I'd love to be part of your process, so don't hesitate to contact me. Perhaps you'll choose to gather with us for the first Superhero Summit (date TBD), or become part of that dream network of 100 independent micro-schools!

Does this all sound enticing? Are you finding yourself wanting to learn more, to become part of this movement to create a new kind of education for today's new kids? There's lots of work to do to prepare you for the adventure that lies ahead. So let's get started!

Chapter 2

WHY Build a School as YOUR Business?

What the best and wisest parent wants for his own child, that must the community want for all its children. Any other ideal for our schools is narrow and unlovely; acted upon, it destroys our democracy.

- John Dewey

I'm hoping that sharing a bit about my micro-school building has helped you feel a connection and to help you begin to hone in on why you want to build a school as your business. As the Dewey quote hints at, building a micro-school for your child may seem a selfish act, but can ultimately have a broader impact upon the children in your community. It's something that you can do for your child to also benefit all children.

Having read the first two chapters of the book, have you figured out some of the connections between us?

- We love working with kids.
- We are passionate about building our own business.
- We want to leave a lasting legacy that makes a difference in the world.
- We know that kids today need something different from education.
- We fantasize about creating a different kind of experience around school for today's amazing kids.

These are powerful reasons to motivate a person to build a school. So now let's address the core question of why YOU would want to build a school.

As author Simon Senek suggests, "why" is one of the most critical questions we must ask ourselves before starting anything that's really important. Most people save the question of why for last, beginning with the who, what, when, where, and how questions first. Starting with the "why" is a strategy that some of the most successful people on the planet utilize to craft a mission with meaning, one that other people can believe in and get behind.

Knowing your "why" first can serve so many purposes. Perhaps most importantly, it's the answer you can offer to all the detractors, naysayers and disbelievers who may come to challenge you. Knowing your "why" in regards to starting a micro-school ahead of time, will also let you easily answer questions such as:

- Start a school, are you crazy?
- Why would you want to start a school?

- Isn't it impossible to open a school with all the regulations?
- Why would you create a school when there is one right down the street?
- Aren't there already enough alternative and private schools out there?
- Why don't you just send your child to X, Y, or Z private school?
- What makes you think you have what it takes to open a school anyway?
- Who do you think you are you to buck the existing system anyway?

If those probing questions didn't make you just a wee bit uncomfortable – YAY! If they did make you think "Yikes what am I doing?" awesome too!

Creating a school isn't a walk in the park, but it isn't climbing Mount Everest either. It's a task, which means it can be broken down into steps or parts. That means with diligence and effort, it can be achieved! So let's start by tackling some of those detractor questions and discover the big reasons why you and I need to engage in the task of creating new schools for today's kids. Here are my top ten reasons why you might choose to build a micro-school.

WHY #1: *Kids today are VERY different than a few generations ago.*

This statement is often true for every generation. It points to the experience of those of us who are a bit older, looking to the younger generations and wondering, what are they thinking? Why are they doing those things? Why do that like particular types of music, clothing, and movies?

It seems that no matter how much time passes, the younger generations always want to start over, do things in their own way, and to innovate. Can you remember being that kind of kid who knew better than the adults, who could see the folly of doing things in the ways that they had always been done just because some adult said so? Perhaps you were the kid who longed for school to be different too. If so, it's time for you to take action!

So how are kids really different today, and how are those differences incompatible with the way school functions? In my first book, *HELP! My Child Hates School,* I spent some significant time describing the ways in which kids are truly different than they were just a few generations ago. Kids today learn, comprehend, and work in ways that are increasingly incompatible with the way schools are set up. So one of your why's can be that kids who are different deserve schools that adapt to what they want and need to thrive as learners.

Most importantly, though, I believe it's time to create settings for learning where wanting to do things differently than past generations is an option. Where kids are encouraged to innovate and create in new ways.

One of the best ways I have found to determine my "why" is to use the vehicle of meditation. As a student of Buddhism and practitioner of mindfulness, I have been taught to focus on the breath, to clear my mind. But a lesser known practice of Vipassana – or "insight" meditation – is to contemplate a question. At many points, I have chosen to sit in meditation with questions related to school, such as:

- Why does school function the way it does?
- What is the real purpose of school?
- Why do so many kids hate school?
- What can I do to help?

By holding these questions in my mind, without seeking to answer them directly, I have had some startling insights. And they have generally come at moments when I wasn't even thinking about them. By meditating on questions of "why," I've come to understand far more about education, its foundations, and new directions we can take, from meditating.

And so, I'd like to offer you a chance to do the same. I'd like to propose a meditation upon your purpose, your *why*, upon the reason you are going to build a micro-school. I have provided a guide below to get you started.

WHY #2: *Because you have had a compelling vision of the kinds of kids you can serve by opening a school.*

Guided Meditation

Let's begin. Find a comfortable chair and make sure that your feet are both flat on the floor. Relax your arms and let your hands rest lightly on your lap. Swing your head back and forth gently to release any tension stored in your neck and shoulders. Now take in a deep breath and hold it in your belly for a moment. Exhale quickly, allowing any tension in your body to exit with the air. Take a few more deep breaths, exhaling any remaining tension you notice in your body.

Now gently let your eyes close. They don't have to be fully closed, but allow your eyelids to relax and soften

47

your gaze so that you aren't looking at anything in particular. Now begin to imagine....

You are sitting in the middle of a room. It is bright and full of light. Your body is relaxed and you feel a sense of deep peace and joy. Let that feeling wash over you and allow you to relax further.

As you continue to sit in this space, breathing in and out, a door opens. In that doorway stands a child. Look closely at the child. Can you tell the child's age, gender, ethnicity? Observe all of the details of the child.

Now reach out your hand to welcome them into the room or motion for the child to join you. Next to you is a chair, so invite the child to sit down next to you.

This is your first student, the child for whom your school is being created.

You may speak to the child or talk with the child by writing on a piece of paper. In this meditation, you may find that you can actually communicate with the child telepathically. You can think of things you'd like to ask the child, and you can hear the child's responses in your mind without any words being spoken.

No matter how you choose to communicate, this child is here to be served by you and the new micro-school you are building. So take time to ask any questions you may have about the child and what they need.

Most importantly, listen carefully to what they child is saying to you, or look at the images the child is creating in your mind.

- Does the child have a known mission they are on that they need your help to fulfill?
- Does the child have special gifts or talents they need support in cultivating?
- Does the child have thoughts about how they would like the school to look, feel, run on a daily basis?

If you can, take some notes about the details being shared by your first student.

As the child finishes sharing with you, thank them for all they've offered. You can hug the child or shake hands as they depart through the same door. Now sit quietly for a few minutes and reflect upon all that the child shared with you.

Return your mind to the same room where you met with the child. Now gently let your eyes begin to move past the door to the surrounding space. Where are you? This is the space created by the child you just met to represent the "school" space for learning.

Notice any details that appear. Are you in a building? Are there walls and windows, a floor and ceiling? What is the building made of, where is it located? Is there furniture? What sort of materials are available? And so on. Allow your mind to envision this learning space and to bask in the details and beauty of the creation. Take note of as much detail as you possibly can.

Now gently imagine yourself standing up from your seat and walking toward the same doorway that the child came through. As you pass through the doorway, allow your mind to come back into your body. Feel your feet on the floor, your hands on your lap. Roll your head gently and feel your neck and shoulders. Take several long slow breaths to ground yourself back into your body. Slowly allow your eyes to open.

When you are ready, write about what you saw and heard. Describe the child you met with, what you talked about, and the details of what the school space looked like. We'll use these details in upcoming exercises, so there is no need to write out your descriptions fully – just jot down the big ideas so that you can keep the image fresh and true.

WHY #3: *YOUR child needs something different.*

One of the big motivators in building a micro-school is *your child or children* needing something not available in any other educational setting. When your child isn't happy in school and you can't locate a school that can serve his or her needs, then it's often time to build the solution yourself.

Once a week I do a Facebook LIVE segment about micro-schools. After one broadcast, I was contacted by Andrea, a full-time engineer and mom of twins. She called because she was considering opening a micro-school of her own.

Knowing that her children needed something different than the local public school, Andrea and her husband did an exhaustive search of small schools in Florida, actually purchasing a home close to a new micro-school they felt would benefit their children. But making the 45-minute drive each way to drop off her children was taking its toll on Andrea. And so she's begun the process of creating a plan to open either a satellite location of her children's school or to open a micro-school of her own from a building she has on her property. In either case, Andrea's priority is making sure that her children receive the attention and focus they need to thrive as learners.

WHY #4: *You engage kids outside of school with amazing content and feel that it should be offered all of the time.*

Another great reason to build a micro-school is that you are already providing amazing content to kids outside of the traditional classroom and school setting.

Perhaps you are an artist or musician who teaches kids privately. You might be someone who runs a robotics or computer program for kids after school. Or maybe you lead an incredible summer camp that has kids coming back year after year to participate in your kid-focused activities. Regardless of your modes and methods, expanding your programming to run 180 days a year as a fully-functioning "school with a theme" is a powerful way to both reach more kids at a deeper level, while also bumping up your potential earning capacity.

Case in point, one of my micro-school building clients, Sophia. For the past 10 years, she has been serving as the chief of staff for a non-profit organization dedicated to empowering the children of tomorrow. The Good Knight Child Empowerment Network (GKCEN) has offered amazing programs both in schools and at their Maryland location, to help kids learn the 10 deceptions that predators use to trick victims. Through a knighting ceremony for those students, the organization empowers them to go out and teach those lessons to other kids too.

GKCEN also hosts a weekly summer day camp at their castle location. Camp WOW (World of Wonders) allows kids to learn deep wisdom about working together in community by giving them freedom to explore, all day, every day. Using the teachings of author Don Miguel Ruiz (*The Four Agreements*), camp staff do most of their direct teaching in the moment as authentic challenges surface. Kids are given time to explore their interests in areas such as art, music, archery, swimming, and more.

Sophia and I are working to craft her action plan to transform the non-profit castle site into a fully-functioning micro-school by the fall of 2018. Much of the learning content and pedagogical practices that are now in place at the summer camp will be morphed into a year-round independent learning center for highly-motivated, spiritual kids.

WHY #5: *Your heart (or dreams) urge you to do this work. You know kids need to follow their own pathway.*

Some of us come to the micro-school building adventure without kids of our own or specific programs we want to expand upon. Perhaps you are someone with a vision of how things might be different for today's kids. If you are anything like me, then you may well have dreams at night about doing something different for kids related to education. If you haven't already created programming for kids, then starting your own micro-school might well be the perfect launching point.

WHY #6: *You've tried lots of things professionally and haven't found your niche yet.*

Lots of us are dabblers and creatives nowadays. So many of us have multiple passions and interests that we find it difficult at times to settle into a career that matches our unique blend of talents. Perhaps we start into a career we think will help us get more money or free time, or will lead us into something more aligned with our hearts.

Many who come to education have this sort of creative servant's heart. Often when folks start with a career that limits their creativity and ability to do something of value that helps kids, they find themselves retraining to become a teacher.

The only problem with this late career switch nowadays is the increasing demands and reduction of time for innovation and creativity in the classroom. While late career educators have SO much to offer in terms of wisdom and experience, they often find it difficult to work under the strict guidelines of standards, curriculum, and assessment.

This is where micro-schools hold so much promise. If you are someone in a career that you no longer love, but with a ton of passion and wisdom to share with kids, then perhaps starting a themed micro-school is just the answer you've been looking for.

WHY #7: *You've always wanted to own your own business (or school).*

Most people don't think of building a school as a business. Far from it, when most of us think of school, we envision large non-profit or tax-funded entities. Micro-schools, however, are a way for today's parents or entrepreneurs to start something meaningful for today's kids while also creating a stable revenue stream for themselves.

We've see this model take hold with day-care providers, test-prep centers, and creative after-school opportunities – why not with school itself? The individualized attention that our kids get when they go to franchised centers for particular instruction is the very same opportunity that is presented to the adult who chooses to open a micro-school as a business.

WHY#8: *There is data that shows smaller classes may be better.*

The Center for Public Education has looked at a large number of studies on the impact of class size and student achievement. Combining many years of research, they have found that class size does, in fact, matter. When it comes to more effective learning, especially with students in grades K-3, the teacher to student ratio should be no more than 1 to 18. And there are those who believe the ratio of 1 to 12 is even better.

Now it's important to note that these numbers related to size are measured against a student's academic achievement: the generally accepted measure of how well a child is doing in school. However, parents who choose to homeschool, unschool, or create a micro-school for their child are usually interested in other measures of growth in kids. Some of the skills being focused on in micro-schools include: the ability to take initiative, open-mindedness, effort, critical thinking, creativity, curiosity, kindness, the ability to love, social and emotional intelligence skills, and more.

It's important to note that these "softer skills" can't be

measured by traditional test-based measures, so if you're interested in including them in your micro-school design, you'll also want to think about how you'll document a child's progress in those areas to show change or growth.

WHY #9: *The Iroquois Confederacy "Seventh Generation Principle"*

Few of us realize that today's modern educational systems have their roots in the not too distant past. Only a few hundred years old at best, our current industrial model of education is often thought to be the gold standard. And yet it remains relatively un-responsive to the rapid change in needs of today's kids.

In Native American traditions, wisdom teachers often share the "seventh generation principle" to guide all planning and decision-making activities. The principle requires that we take into account the impact of our decisions upon the next seven generations. Because that principle asks us to make choices about children we'll never meet, facing challenges we'll never know, it requires that we think both conservatively as well as with great foresight and flexibility.

I personally believe, and hope you will too, that micro-schools are one way to do that. In the coming chapters, we will talk about the big foundational blocks needed to build a micro-school. Creating processes and procedures that are simple and agile, you'll be able to pivot around kids' needs as well as changes in the economy, environment, or community, allowing you to potentially think seven generations forward.

Now that we've touched on some of the potential "why's" for you to build a micro-school, let's do a litmus test. Do you believe that you are you ready to tackle the process from start to finish? Ask yourself the following questions:

• Do you have sufficient motivation to build a school?
• Do you have the heart to serve today's amazing kids?
• Do you have the determination to see the process from start to finish?

If the answers were yes, then let's get started. While the task of building a school is large, I'm here to help break it down into a simpler set of steps. The process I will guide you through in rest of the book will help you to create your very own plan of action. It includes 8 foundational building blocks you will need to build the school of your dreams.

Before we move on to the first building block, I'd like to share a short story with you. It's about building a school as a gift to humanity, as a unique legacy.

In 1921, A.S. Neil opened his British independent boarding school, Summerhill, around the notion that a school should fit children's needs and desires, not the other way around. Amazingly, nearly 100 years later Summerhill is still in operation, run as a democratic school. It's one of the longest running and best-known examples of alternative education. (You can read more about democratic schools in upcoming chapters and by searching for those topics online.)

Like many parents, A.S. Neil was dissatisfied with the educational options he could see, and so he began a search for alternatives. And as many of you will do, Neil read extensively and visited as many different independent schools as he could, taking note of the processes and ideas which resonated with him.

Summerhill has functioned on Neil's premise of "Freedom, not license" – the notion of the freedom to explore one's interests and to exercise them, while also learning to be part of community and caring for others. Summerhill has faced a wide variety of challenges to these ideas over the years. The most intense came when the Office for Standards in Education listed Summerhill on a watch list, and criticized the school's belief that children will come to learning when they are ready. (One of Summerhill's core practices is to reject the practice of compulsory education, allowing students to come to class when they are ready.) Summerhill staff, and the students, rallied and secured legal counsel. After four days in court, the state settled the case, and students utilized their democratic training to discuss the terms in the settlement. Ultimately the students and staff chose to accept the settlement, and the school continues to flourish today.

One of the pieces of the story – which isn't generally highlighted as important – is A.S. Neil's daughter's part in the longevity of the school. Zoe Redhead attended Summerhill as a student and then went on to lead the school, after her mother retired in 1985. While the stories told about Summerhill over the years are sometimes fantastical, what I am most impressed with is the school's longevity and its legacy.

As you begin to craft your plan for building a microschool, you'll want to consider the notion of longevity and legacy. Who will continue to run the school when you are gone? Certainly if you have a child who grows up in the school, the possibility of passing down your school to your child in adulthood is there. But what if your child chooses another pathway? Who will carry the vision forward for the next seven generations? With those kinds of questions in your mind, you have a much better chance of sustaining the impact and legacy your micro-school has to offer the world.

To wrap up this chapter, I offer one more "why" for your consideration.

Why #10: *Who are you NOT to open a school?*

In her book, *A Return to Love: Reflections on the Principles of "A Course in Miracles,* author Marianne Williamson says:

> Our deepest fear is not that we are inadequate. Our deepest fear is that we are powerful beyond measure. It is our light, not our darkness, that most frightens us. We ask ourselves, 'Who am I to be brilliant, gorgeous, talented, fabulous?' Actually, who are you not to be? You are a child of God. Your playing small does not serve the world. There is nothing enlightened about shrinking so that other people won't feel insecure around you. We are all meant to shine, as children do. We were born to make manifest the glory of God that is within us. It's not just in some of us; it's in everyone. And as we let our own light shine, we unconsciously give other people permission to do the same. As we are liberated from our own fear, our presence automatically liberates others.

To me, Williamson speaks to the "why" of building micro-schools in such an eloquent way. We can talk ourselves out of the task at any point along the path. But knowing that it is just fear of success that lies behind our hiding can help.

And so I ask you...

Who are you to not open a school that makes a huge difference in your own child's and hundreds of other children's lives?

If you need help, or want to talk this question through, I'm ready to listen. And I'm also here to serve as your guide on this grand adventure. Let's begin!

Chapter 3

Building Block #1 – Frame your WHY with a PLAN

Education is the passport to the future,
for tomorrow belongs to those who prepare for it today.

- Malcom X

If you haven't done so already, I recommend you start taking notes to gather your ideas in one place. It may work well to take your notes in digital form, allowing you to quickly copy and paste them down the road. If you are more the journal type, that works too. As you continue to read ahead, I'll be asking lots of questions, suggesting research you'll want to do, and helping you to consider ideas which might fit into your micro-school plan. Taking notes as you go along will be truly helpful when it comes time to pull your ideas together into a business plan towards the end of the book.

In the last chapter I shared 10 potential "whys" that might motivate your micro-school building plan. Now we need to hone in on your why. And it's time we begin to craft a plan to support all of the steps that you'll need to make to turn that why into a fully functioning micro-school designed for your kids.

Just to refresh your memory, your "why" can contain a motivation such as:

- You feel a calling to serve children to help them grow to their highest potential.
- You want to create a different educational experience from the one you grew up with.
- You have ideas about how to make school more fun and engaging.
- You want to create a business for yourself that allows you to be with your kids all day.
- You have had a dream or a vision about creating a school that doesn't go away.

Part of what we need to do now is to stitch together your "why" with an actual plan that you can share with the world. You'll need a plan to help you talk with prospective parents and students. If you want to have staff who do the teaching in your school, a plan will help you find the perfect employees. You'll likely want to secure some funding for your school and a sound plan will allow you to shop the idea to investors, funders, or lenders. It's also a tool you'll use to build your action plan at the end of the book.

As you continue to contemplate your "why," perhaps you'd like to hear the stories of why a few of my friends and clients have chosen to build their micro-schools.

I first met Lisa through via a connection from a friend and fellow author. After a few exchanged messages, Lisa and I scheduled time to talk. In our first meeting, we both felt like it was a meeting of the minds. We had both worked as teachers and had gone on to earn advanced degrees in education. Where my path had led me into teacher training for in-service teachers and administration, Lisa's path had taken her into a teacher preparation at the undergraduate level.

With the birth of her son, Lisa began the journey that so many of you share. Her son, medically fragile, had many challenges once he entered school. Lisa didn't immediately know that his issues with emotional control and self-regulation were related to diet and environmental irritants. After much research, many visits to the doctors, and way too many visits to the school to try to advocate for her son's needs, Lisa realized that home-schooling was the only way she could ensure her son receive the education he both needed and craved. After a few months of balancing her son's education with her college classes in education, Lisa had an ah-ha moment. She realized that with all of her knowledge about personalized, hands-on, and authentic learning, she could open a school for her son.

Lisa framed her ideas about where the school would be located, how it would function, how students would learn, and what it would cost, over a long weekend. Then she began to talk with her closest friends about the idea, and within a few short weeks, she convened a small gathering to talk about the idea further. They quickly drafted up a plan, much like you will be doing as you read this book. Once complete, Lisa shared it with her closest family, friends, and a few young educators she knew.

Quickly her ideas generated excitement and momentum. Teams began to form and within six months, Lisa and her collaborators were launching a summer program to help acclimate the new students to the world of her micro-school. From start to finish, Lisa was able to get her micro-school up and off the ground with 17 students enrolled, in less than a year.

I'm happy to report that Lisa's son is happy and flourishing in the school, and she has found a way to balance her administration and oversight of the new micro-school while also maintaining her faculty status at the university.

Sophia and I met when I was completing my first book about what to do when your child hates school. We were introduced by my book coach, Angela, as she recognized the potential that a collaboration between us might offer. Her son Jesse had been attending summer camp under Sophia's guidance for the past six years.

In my introduction to you around my work I shared a bit about my client Sophia's non-profit work. I'm happy to report that at the completion of the writing of this book, Sophia is most of the way through the creation of her business plan. We have initial meetings scheduled with local parents to share the vision and mission, and to begin the process of finding collaborators, students, and teachers. With approximately seven months to get the school model in place before a fall 2018 launch, Sophia is easily on track to launch her school with a handful of learners who crave independence and mentorship to guide their immense curiosity as the main vehicle for their learning.

The steps that both Lisa and Sophia took are like building blocks. Each has some weight to it, and each has a separate function in laying the foundation for the school. The actual shape, form, and flavor of their two schools may be significantly different from yours, but their process is very similar. Their process and yours is like any journey; it has its complexities. But by laying out the road that lies ahead in eight action steps, or building blocks, I am confident that you too can create your plan of action quickly and easily.

The building blocks you will create in this process do not necessarily have to be completed in a linear fashion. That is, you can take a look at the list of building blocks and then choose to tackle them in an order that suits you, using your vision and your style. In the end, you'll need all eight pieces in order to complete your plan and get going on building the micro-school of your dreams. The order that you lay the foundational blocks should make sense for you.

To whet your appetite, here's an overview of those eight building blocks in the micro-school building process:

- Building Block #1 - Frame Your WHY with a PLAN
- Building Block #2 - Get Legalities Out of the Way!
- Building Block #3 - What's YOUR Special Sauce?
- Building Block #4 - Location, Location, Location
- Building Block #5 - Show Me the Money!
- Building Block #6 - David vs. Goliath
- Building Block #7 - People, People, People
- Building Block #8 - Ready, Set, GO!

A lot of what we'll cover in the following chapters may remind you of creating a traditional business plan. And that's because all of the elements we'll craft are ones you'll need to actually get a business plan done for your micro-school. Hopefully the process will feel fun and easy as we do it, and assembling the elements together in a usable, marketable, business plan will feel effort-less!

Here's a little more detail about what to expect in each of the chapters to come:

Building Block #1 – Frame Your WHY with a PLAN

In this current chapter, we are making sense of micro-school building as a process that requires a strategy and a plan to make things happen. We will lay out the framework that will guide the entire micro-school build-ing process.

Building Block #2 – Get Legalities Out of the Way!

In this chapter, we will talk about the various stances a micro-school can take legally. Because micro-school building is a movement to liberate learners globally, we need to know how to find the legislation around educa-tion where we live, and determine what methods fit within those statutes. If that sounds scary, not to worry. We've got lots of resources to help and pointers out to some great legal advice that you can get for free or at low cost to you as you work through the process.

In this chapter we'll also touch on insurance, policies, forms, clearances, and more. All those little "detail" items that seem to sneak up on us when we aren't aware of what they are, why they are needed, and when to put them in place.

Building Block #3 – What's YOUR Special Sauce?

In this chapter, we will dream up your school, its vision, mission, and how things will run on a daily, weekly, monthly, and annual basis. You'll think about who will be responsible for what, how decisions will be made, and the roles that everyone will take both before, during, and after the launch of your micro-school.

Building Block #4 – Location, Location, Location

In this chapter, we'll talk about where your school will live. We'll look at topics like renting space, bartering for space, buying a building, building a structure from the ground up, sharing space, utilizing your own space, having no building at all, and more! We'll also talk a bit about the importance of space as a key determinant in how your school functions, as well as its impact upon the students you serve.

Building Block #5 – Show Me the Money!

In this chapter, we will examine topics of funding. We'll start by looking at why micro-schools are so powerful – because they ignore the traditional forms of "who holds the bag of money" syndrome. We'll look at where to look for start-up funds, doing fundraisers and crowd-funding, and looking for angel donors or investors. We'll touch on salaries, ongoing expenses related to operations, and even how you can build a revenue generation stream within the school. Finally, we'll touch on the considerations you'll need to make regarding for profit or non-profit status (functioning as an LLC, S. Corp., or 501c3), and how to document income and expenditures for tax purposes.

Building Block #6 - David vs. Goliath

In this chapter, we'll talk about how and what kids will learn in your school. We'll explore the difference between knowledge and wisdom and tie the concepts to what kids today really want from an education. We'll slay the notion of "curriculum" by looking at how your school can innovate using techniques borrowed from the homeschooling, unschooling, road-schooling, and world-schooling movements.

Building Block #7 – People, People, People

In this chapter, we'll talk about all of the stakeholders you'll need to define and locate related to your school. From the parents who send their children to your school, to the adults who provide learning support, to your role as the visionary and owner of the school, there are many hats to be worn. We'll talk about the difference between teachers and learning facilitators, and we'll focus in on mentors and partnerships to add richness to your special sauce. You will decide how you envision your school being run (top down, bottom up, other?), who will make decisions, whether you believe in power vs. authority, how you envision parents' role in the school, and where you'll look for help along the way. And finally, we'll lay out the big categories of people and define each as part of your plan.

Building Block #8 – Ready, Set, GO!

In this final building block chapter, we will take a look at all that you've created so far. To get READY, we'll pull it all together into one nice, neat document – a business plan. To get SET: We'll talk about what to do with the plan – how to share it, organize meetings, and recruit partners. And we'll also cover the addition of a timeline to the end of the document to guide your steps moving forward in putting the plan into motion for real. And to GO, we'll lay out a plan for what the launch of your school might look like in the first day, week, month, and year. We'll wrap up this final building block chapter with a brief look at longevity.

Chapter 4

Building Block #2 – Get Legalities Out of the Way!

Education is for improving the lives of others
and for leaving your community and world better than
you found it.

- Marian Wright Edelman

Wow, I can almost hear you screaming. Legal stuff. YUK!

For many, legal issues are the biggest pain point in the whole micro-school planning and building process. Yet knowing the legal statutes in your location regarding the opening of a school of any kind is a critical step in the process, so we are going to tackle the topic head on, up front, and get it out of the way.

The first place to begin is to consider whether or not you would like to open your school under the umbrella of the big system of education or not. In case you aren't sure, I'll walk you through a bit of my own personal thinking around the pros and cons of both.

Opening a Charter School

If you are living in the United States and are interested in opening a school that receives public funds, from the collection of property taxes in many cases, then you would legally need to apply for a charter. While this isn't an option in all 50 of the United States, or in many countries across the globe, there is an increasing push to make charter schools legal everywhere to allow innovators to use government funding in ways that can make a difference. The pluses to going this route are guaranteed funds once your charter is approved. If you go into the planning process knowing the amount of funds you'd be eligible for, per student, you can make some clear and logical budgetary decisions about resources, materials, and staff. The main drawbacks to opening a charter school, in my opinion, are all of the requirements that come along with the funding.

From direct evaluation or oversight from departments of education, to requirements to utilize state standards or to conduct standardized assessments, the amount of control placed upon you, your staff, and students may be something to consider before going down this road. So many of the issues that appear in our public schools today stem from students feeling overburdened by content memorization, grading, and testing. Students are being asked to take in content and to spit it back out for tests. If you go the route of opening a charter school, you may well be signing up for a continuation of at least some of those priorities which make public school less enjoyable for children.

To open a charter school, you'll have to investigate the charter laws in your state to determine the specific timelines and processes. An internet search for keywords such as: open a charter school in my state, charter school laws, and so on, will get you started.

In general, most charter schools take a minimum of two years to open their doors. The amount of time and energy that you will need to spend in preparing the application to the local district granting the charter can be quite extensive. And in many cases, it is expected that you have all of your ducks in a row ahead of time, in terms of location, staff, curriculum, and students. In most cases, you'll need to have to have your school ready to go, at least on a small scale, in order to get your charter school licensing approved.

Here's a bit of tough news. It's important to know up front that in nearly all cases, your charter school application will be automatically rejected by a school district, regardless of your plan's merit. If you think about it, it kind of makes sense. Here you are asking to take away some of the school district's precious budgetary funds to do something different from what the school district already provides. Not only are you potentially cutting into the budget, but you are also putting the district's enrollment numbers at risk. You are appearing as direct competition for limited resources. And so many school districts are already running at a deficit because of state and federal cut backs, that many are on the defensive from the start.

Just knowing ahead of time that your application has a high likelihood of rejection will give you the opportunity to move forward with a charter school application in a more mindful way. Expecting for the application to take time will help. You'll be able to craft a realistic plan for how you'll take care of your basic needs during the two-year time frame. And you'll have an idea of how to handle the initial rejection should it come. You'll have a strategy in place for going right back in and applying to the next level of officials for a reconsideration right away. Knowing that the payoff may take time can also help you focus on offering something truly unique. Serving kids a school district can't handle is another way to make them your friend versus your adversary.

Opening a Private School

If you find strict adherence to state or national standards and the intense focus on assessment to be less enticing, but still want the ability to offer your students an "approved program," you may wind up choosing to go the route of applying for private school status. Searching the internet for phrases such as: open a private school, and private school law, will help you to locate the particular regulations to be followed in your state, province, or country. Private school regulations vary widely in the US. In some states, one can literally open a private school with little or no fanfare, while in others, a private school designation requires a founder to not only have a business plan completed, but the majority of resources needed already gathered and ready to go.

Starting Small

In the case of both charter or private school status, my strongest recommendation is to follow a third, different pathway to begin. After you have a bit of time and experience under your belt, you can consider the pros and cons to becoming a legally recognized school under either the public or private system. You'll have something to show, and enough experience with the processes, that the application and vetting processes will be a breeze.

There are some real advantages to making your own way. One is the freedom you'll gain in keeping out from under various regulations. Another is the ability to remain small and agile. Working with a smaller number of students in a flexible and responsive manner will allow you to customize and personalize learning for your students. This is actually a very attractive feature of micro-schools, and one that many parents are willing to pay handsomely for.

Some of the ways in which today's micro-school builder situates their school are to function, at least early on, as:

- a homeschool resource center
- a cyber-school resource center
- a tutoring center
- a co-working/learning space with room for adults to have their children work on homeschooling or cyber content while they are conducting business

Homeschool Resource Center

A homeschool resource center is somewhat like a homeschooling cooperative. Its biggest difference lies in its ability to take over some of the responsibilities for children's learning when parents need to be away doing other things. It's one of the ways a homeschooling parent can generate revenue while legally homeschooling their own child. You'll want to check state regulations to determine how often you can offer homeschooling support to another parent's child. In some states, provinces, and countries, there are laws governing the number of children you can serve.

Cyber-School Resource Center

A cyber-school resource center is a place for kids enrolled in an online learning platform to gather, collaborate, be supported, and spend time with peers. One of the downfalls of cyber-schooling is the isolation some kids experience. Cyber resource centers also allow parents who want their child to be cyber-schooled to get help in making sure that their child is on task each day, offering freedom to tend to other priorities.

Tutoring Center

A tutoring center is another way to get your micro-school going. Offering individualized and customized learning to a small number of children, it's an option that most of us think is only available to the very wealthy. Today this option can be made available to small groups of kids. Be sure to check out the regulations in your state, province, or country to know how many children you can tutor at one time, and for what length of time.

Shared Working/Learning Space

And finally, the newest configuration for some micro-school owners is to create a co-working space. These shared spaces are all the rage in many big cities nowa-days, and more and more of them are beginning to understand the value of offering educational options for their clients' children. Parents can not only get the connections and resources they need to get their own business off the ground, they can have their kids nearby while they are working. There is something special that happens when a child is able to see his mom or dad as an entrepreneur in action, hence the attraction to so many young, business-minded parents. If this configuration interests you, you'll want to consider having attending students designated as homeschoolers or cyber students. If your participating parents want their students to be homeschooled, "road-schooled," or "world-schooled," then you'll need to make sure they've properly signed their children out of the traditional systems.

If you choose to explore any of the configurations described above, it's important to review regulations. Just as you did a search for terms around how to open a private or charter school, you'll need to look for answers about the homeschool regulations in your state, province, or country. Again, just as we saw with school licensure, homeschool laws vary widely.

In some states in the US, parents only need to inform their local school district that they are going to home-school their child. In far more, however, this notification comes with some sort of guidelines to be followed in regards to what the student is to learn during the year, how that learning is to be documented, and how the work will be reviewed by the granting agency to ensure that the child has made growth academically.

One of the best resources out there in regards to navigating the laws around homeschooling is a website created by the Homeschool Legal Defense Association (HSLDA). Founded in 1983 by two attorneys who were also homeschooling dads, the website is a treasure trove of information about the latest legal challenges to alternative forms of education. One of the best resources on the website is their homeschool law map. It will help you quickly determine the regulations for your state, and what the law will allow in regards to positioning your students as homeschoolers.

Once you have determined your stance, whether you'll function as a homeschool resource center, cyber center, tutoring center, shared working/learning center, or some hybrid of those forms, you'll need to consider other legal matters.

In opening a school, you'll want to decide the legal format your business will take. Will you choose to function as a:

- non-profit (501c3)
- for-profit (LLC or S-Corp)

There are several good reasons for positioning as a non-profit, and others for functioning as a for-profit. I have my personal opinions on the matter and will share them in a bit. But first, let's take a look at the difference between the two legal statuses for your micro-school.

Non-Profit

Generally when we think of schools, we think of them as non-profit entities. This is because our public schools function based on tax revenues (in general) and so there is no desire to generate extra revenue beyond what is provided by the local government. This is beginning to shift slightly in public schools, however, as government budgets are cut and staff are reduced to the bone. Many schools are now in the business of generating extra revenue to cover costs, and parents are increasingly being asked to pick up the burden of any items or activities deemed to be extracurricular.

The main reason many micro-school builders decide to apply for 501c3 non-profit status is because of the opportunity to take donations which are tax deductible. In order to keep tuitions at a more manageable level, many micro-schools run fundraising campaigns and offer donors the benefit of a tax deductible donation toward capital improvement projects, tuition banks, and extra-curricular activities.

One of the real drawbacks to forming as a non-profit is the requirement to recruit and convene a governing board of directors. With so many of us busy already with work and family life, fewer and fewer people are willing to offer up their time (and money – most non-profit boards expect their members to make donations) to serve on a non-profit board. Not only that, there are the considerations of input to take into account. In some cases, you can launch your school with a clear vision and mission, and over time, the board can begin to erode or even undermine the school's original purpose. So if you go this route, you'll want to consider recruiting a small board of directors who truly share your purpose, mission, and vision around the micro-school to ensure its longevity.

For-Profit

Surprisingly, more and more micro-school builders are choosing to position themselves as a for-profit entity. There are several reasons for that change in direction. In the previous section, we talked about the impact board members with differing ideas can have upon your micro-school's vision and mission. In some drastic cases, a school's main founders have even been ousted by a board that no longer shared the same vision or goals for the school. In one case I've read about, the ousted founder of the school regrouped, and reopened a school with for-profit status. We will want to avoid that kind of challenge for you, so let's talk about some of the benefits to setting up as a for-profit micro-school.

Perhaps the simplest reason why you might want to consider functioning as a for-profit is that you retain more control and influence over the school. You are the school's owner, you make the decisions, you hire and fire staff, you select the students who attend, you charge the tuition that meets your needs and goals. In the case of wanting the ability to take donations from people aligned with your mission, you can seek out a non-profit partner and create a cooperative relationship which benefits you both.

Case in point. In an earlier chapter, I described the potential school partnership I formed with a non-profit community center in Virginia. By situating the micro-school as a for-profit business, we would have fit into the center's model – it was a central location where small businesses could rent space and do collaborative marketing of their goods and services. It just so happened that the non-profit center had a large portion of its mission focused on education. By opening up a micro-school in the center, our school would have not only benefitted from low costs related to securing learning space, but we would, in turn, have nearly met all of the non-profits goals related to its educational initiatives. It was a win-win, so to speak, for both of us.

In your situation, you might look for a similar non-profit with a building and the ability to handle your charitable donations towards tuition and materials. You can offer rent back to the non-profit from the tuition you collect, and both you and the non-profit benefit. Lots of micro-schools make their humble beginnings in this way – and many of them find a safe haven under the umbrella of such an organization. One obvious choice is to see if a local church is willing to let you rent space, in return for its acting as your non-profit partner.

Once you have chosen how to situate your school legally, you'll want to go about the task of filing for the chosen status. In the case of creating an LLC or S Corporation to serve as your for-profit entity, you can go to your local library and find information on how to complete those applications. Another route to go is to search the internet for support in creating your LLC. This is one of those times you may want to consider consulting with a lawyer. No amount of web-based content can replace the attention and hand holding you get from a lawyer in making some potentially complicated decisions. If you simply must utilize an online resource, then check out CorpNet.com for business information.

If you choose to go the non-profit route, you can learn more about non-profits by visiting the IRS's website and free publication here: https://www.irs.gov/publications/p557. And again, consider securing the services of a lawyer familiar with school law to ensure your business is set up properly in your state, province, or country.

So, to review a few of the points we've covered so far, the benefits to setting your school up as a non-profit can include:

- certain tax breaks for state, federal, and other income taxes
- operate as a 501c3, offering tax breaks on certain kinds of charitable donations to your school
- protect your personal assets, as members of a non-profit and its board of directors are shielded from personal liability for the non-profit's actions
- and potential eligibility for grants and donations from government agencies

Whichever way you go, take your time with this part of the process. Know the ins and outs, and choose the plan that feels best to you. Seek out legal counsel to make sure that your business is set upon a strong foundation.

Insurance

Another legal aspect you'll need to tackle in starting your micro-school is insurance. You'll need to carry both personal liability insurance as well as property insurance, especially if you are utilizing your own building. If you are partnering with a business owner or non-profit organization to share space, you'll need to find out what sort of liability insurance they carry to make sure that you are properly covered. In most cases, it's best to seek legal counsel before taking the plunge.

In preparing this book for publication, I sought the legal counsel of fellow author and lawyer (with many years of experience in school law) Beverly Davidek, Esq. Her recommendation was that you all consider purchasing a good umbrella policy and/or life and disability insurance, prior to launching your micro-school.

Her wisdom really struck a chord in me. She said, "Mara, your clients are going to go through all the effort to build a school. What if the owner of the micro-school is sued (even for something complete unrelated to the school), or is injured or dies? How will the school continue to function if something happens to the person at the top? This can be a make-or-break proposition, as it is for other solo or small businesses."

My mission is to help you create the school of your and your child's dreams. I don't want to see anything get in your way. A good insurance policy will help to ensure your dreams do come true!

Clearances

Most states, provinces, and countries require adults who work with children to provide proof that they are fit for the task of serving one of our most precious resources. Before you hire any employees for your micro-school, you'll want to ask applicants to provide you with up to date clearances, including: a criminal history check, child abuse clearances, and fingerprinting. These clearances need to be kept up to date, according to your local governing body, and don't forget, as the owner of the school, you'll need to keep copies of your clearances as well.

Forms, Policies & Procedures

If you've got children in a local public or private school, or know families with kids in school these days, you're likely familiar with the paperwork that comes home from school on a regular basis. At the start of the year, most schools send home forms that not only gather critical contact information, but also articulate school policies. These documents often take the form of a "Student Handbook."

The big items you will find in these kinds of documents include: student/parent rights and responsibilities, employment practices, community considerations, non-discrimination policies, anti-bullying or harassment policies, and everything else in-between. While these things are strongly recommended, they are items that can be created closer to the time you launch your school. In the case of the student responsibilities, many micro-school founders actually engage their students in a discussion of said policies, employing a democratic process in creating the school's code of conduct and grievance procedures.

While not mission critical as you lay out the plan for your school, these documents are an item to keep an eye out for. Ask friends and families to share copies of their school handbooks, policies, and forms with you as you see the opportunity. Check out the website of a local school district and download any of the policies you see online as models. And when you pay a visit to an alternative school, ask to see theirs as well. In many cases, you'll even find that the director of the school is willing to share the files with you digitally, allowing you to utilize the items that work for you, eliminating the need to create everything from scratch.

Agreements

As you begin to consider the location of your school, hiring employees, and collaborating with a friend or investor in a joint venture, you'll need to consider having agreements drafted. These can take the form of lease agreements, employment agreements, or joint venture agreements. And if you are collaborating with a friend or colleague, a buy/sell agreement might be a good idea going into the partnership.

Even if you are working from your own space, teaching the students yourself, and owning the business as a sole proprietor, keep these items in mind. If you have a chance to ask a local alternative school to share these documents with you, alongside the forms, you'll be 10 steps ahead of the game.

Finance

In wrapping up this chapter on legal considerations for your micro-school, we need to briefly touch on issues related to finance. We'll cover much more detail about money in Chapter 7: Show Me the Money! But for now, know that keeping a clear accounting of the money coming in and out of your micro-school will be a critical task. It's something that you as the school founder and potential owner must consider. And it's something you absolutely can find a volunteer or hire an employee to tend to.

Chapter 5

Building Block #3 – What's YOUR Special Sauce?

If you do follow your bliss, you put yourself on a kind of track that has been there all the while, waiting for you, and the life that you ought to be living is the one you are living. Follow your bliss and don't be afraid, and doors will open where you didn't know they were going to be.

— Joseph Campbell

Now that we've explored the legal impacts of state, provincial, or country regulations on your micro-school, it's time to get to the fun stuff. We are going to define YOUR vision a bit further to identify the ingredients in "Your Special Sauce." To do that, we need to take a look at, and gather inspiration from, some of the best models out there.

Explore Existing Models

To begin, let's start with a quick overview of the existing models of alternative education. Because, if you want to jumpstart your process, it's possible to adopt an existing model and shortcut some of the legal red tape. By knowing about what other models have done and how they have approached various matters, you'll be saving yourself time and perhaps money. Not only that, by knowing some of the key components utilized by the most successful schools, you'll save time later on in the other parts of this planning process as well.

Let's step back in time for a moment. The "alternative schools movement," sometimes also referred to as the "free school movement," began in the United States in the 1960s. The movement continued to flourish into the 70s, as many individuals sought to reform education through the creation of independently run community schools. The roots of the movement, though, are much older. Educational philosophers, such as Francisco Ferrer, Homer Lane, and John Holt, each made their mark with bold ideas about student-centered learning.

Some of the new types of schools that flourished in the 60s and 70s included: democratic schools, free schools, Montessori, Waldorf, and Reggio Amelia schools. Each of those schools had a particular vision and mission to guide the work done with students. Below, we'll take a brief look at each of these types of schools. If any of them are new to you, I recommend a little light research. Each of the models has a founder or philosopher who inspired the model's inception. Nearly all have had books written about them which can be purchased online or found in your local library.

The democratic and free schools, typified by schools like Summerhill in England, and the Sudbury School in Massachusetts, focus on the utilization of the democratic process and Socratic methods to empower students as learners. In many of these schools, students are not required to attend classes, but rather to become part of democratic processes which create opportunities for students to choose their own learning pathways at their own pace.

The Montessori, Waldorf, and Reggio Amelia schools – inspired by educational innovators Maria Montessori, Rudolf Steiner, and Loris Malaguzzi respectively in Europe – focus more on the whole child as a learning agent. Encouraging hands-on and participatory activities, these schools seek to engage the creativity of a child to encourage and stimulate his natural learning processes.

One of the oldest and still flourishing original schools is A.S. Neil's Summerhill in England. Founding it in 1924, Neil created a school dedicated to allowing children to have the time, space, and freedom to explore ideas which interested them, and opportunity to work without coercion or fear from retribution from adults. His ideas were radical, and the school has faced numerous challenges to its methods and curriculum over the years. However, over 90 years later, the school is still open and thriving.

Summerhill is an interesting study on a number of levels. Legally, they have faced direct challenge from government around their unusual curriculum and teaching methods. Summerhill staff have made sure that their methods work within the letter of the law, and have secured counsel when needed to make their case in court. Part of Summerhill's success also comes from its legacy – Neil's daughter Zoe Redhead continues to function as the school's director, continuing the vision. If you are building your school as a legacy for your child, then the possibility of continuing the work through him or her holds so much potential for success.

Identify Local Alternative Schools

The next way to get ideas about how you might differentiate your micro-school is to do some light research on alternatives in your vicinity. It's great to not only know what's already out there, so that you don't duplicate services or create competition, but it's also a wonderful way to get support and ideas from others who've been in your shoes not so long ago. I suggest that you make yourself a spreadsheet with the various schools, their location and contact information, a summary of their mission/vision, a link to their website, and the founder or director's name and contact info.

Prior to beginning to advertise for your students, you may want to call each director and share your plans. Convening a gathering of each school's leadership team might also be of great benefit. Talk through ideas around collaboration and sharing of school events. Discuss ways you can refer families to one another when a different setting feels appropriate for a student. This kind of early collaboration should serve you well both during the planning stages and well beyond the launch of your micro-school.

Also plan to schedule a visit to at least one alternative or micro-school you've located and come armed with all of your questions. Plan to spend time watching how the school runs, who leads the learning, how the students interact with one another and the adults, etc. You are sure to get lots of ideas for your school. And be sure to schedule some time with the school's founder if you can. He or she will be the vision keeper, just as you are, and will be able to help "kick the tires" so to speak on the beginnings of your WHY and your ideas about what you might like to accomplish with your micro-school.

In my own micro-school building efforts, I can recall a long conversation with the founder of a small alternative school about five miles from my clients' proposed micro-school location. She shared so much wisdom about how she found her families, gained allies, and tended to the myriad of issues that come up in the early start-up process. Because we were making it a point to offer a school option for students she wasn't able to serve in her K-8 building (who were students moving into high school), she was more than willing to help us promote the idea, both to the community and to her own students and staff!

Explore the New Movements

In the world of alternative education, there are a whole new class of opportunities to educate a child, minus the formal structures of school. Some of the ideas found in these "movements" are innovative and unique. And many of them can be incorporated into your micro-school plan. While the four movements described below often incorporate gatherings to bring kids together for learning, activities, and socialization, they often necessitate your child working in isolation, at least a good bit of the week. In building a micro-school, you can build in the innovation and freedom of the movements, while also offering your child, and other kids like him, the chance to work in community, all day, every day!

Here is a brief description of each movement and its key characteristics. If you find any of interest, I encourage you to do a bit of research to learn more.

Homeschooling

Fairly well known these days, homeschooling, sometimes referred to as "home education," is based upon the notion of educating children inside the home. The learning activities are usually conducted by a parent or tutor. Prior to compulsory education laws, homeschooling was the norm. Homeschooling is a legal alternative to public or private education in many nations. John Holt, considered by many to be the grandfather of the homeschooling movement, believed that homeschooling families should not just replicate a school construct in the home, but rather allow learning to occur as a natural part of daily life.

Unschooling

Similar to homeschooling, unschooling is a philosophy that urges learner-selected activities as the main vehicle for learning. Unschooled students learn through play, internships, work, chores, mentors, family members, books, travel and more. There is a shared belief by unschooling families that the more personalized the experience, the more meaningful learning will take place. One key idea in unschooling is that mastery of content knowledge is less important than learning HOW to learn. The term unschooling was coined by author and homeschooling advocate, John Holt.

Road-Schooling and World-Schooling

These two movements are spin-offs of the homeschooling and unschooling movements. Like their predecessors, they value the input of the child and his experiences, as the main motivators for learning. Road-schooling and world-schooling, as their names imply, utilize the notion of travel as a vehicle for learning. There are many online groups devoted to connecting families on the road, both locally and globally, to bring students together to share learning, to collaborate, and to celebrate.

What all four of these movement have in common is the focus on the student first. Hopefully your explorations into the four movements has given you inspiration around mentorship, apprenticeship, student-generated learning topics, and travel as mechanisms to excite and motivate student learners. By utilizing some of these ideas in the formation of your micro-school, you can offer your child – and your student base – rich and rewarding learning experiences.

Define Your Leadership Role & Governance

Now that we have explored some of the existing models and you've done some research about what kind of schools already exist in your vicinity, it's time to craft your ideas. Remember, it's a great idea to borrow the best from the best.

Start with leadership. How do you envision the leadership structures in your school? Do you believe in a single leader, shared decision-making, democratic processes, or something else? What role will the adults play? Will they function as traditional teachers, instructing students in content? Or will they act more as mentors, guiding students' independent investigations? This is the time to start outlining the governance for your school.

Next up let's think about what you already do and how it can be incorporated into the school of your dreams. Take some time and make a list of all the things that you love to do, love to share with others, love to teach. Are they thematic? Are they things you've shared with kids before? Could they create a particular flavor for your school?

My school building client, Sophia, is a holistic healer, reiki master, and spiritual teacher. In laying out her micro-school plan, she has determined that she will function as the director for the school. She'll offer oversight and guidance for all of the daily activities students participate in, she'll hire teachers, and she'll assign duties to the other staff she employs where needed. She believes that her student body will be made up of kids who aspire to be healers as well, and so she plans to offer herself as a mentor in those areas as the students' interests dictate. And as far as governance and structure goes, because of the non-profit's focus around the knighthood, much of the decision making will happen around the organization's round table, using a shared decision-making process.

Envision an Ideal Day/Month/Year

Next let's think about what sort of calendar year your school will utilize. Will you follow the traditional model of school, engaging students in classes during the late summer through spring, offering a long summer vacation? Will you adopt a 180-day school year? Will your students follow a cycle of nine weeks of class with three weeks off in-between?

What time will students begin classes in the morning and what time will instruction end? Will your students take set courses during specific times of the day or will instruction flow to meet the needs of students? Will academic learning happen in the morning and creative project work in the afternoon? These are all considerations to sketch out as part of your defining "your special sauce."

As you were exploring the existing models and local alternatives in your area, you likely learned more about each school's schedule. What inspired you? What did you think you'd do differently? Take some time to list out how you think you'll manage the day to day processes of student learning.

Describe Your Model

Now that you have looked at existing models and thought about your own skill sets and abilities, take some time to outline your model. Describe the school year in ways that will make sense to a parent who is considering sending their child to your school.

The way in which most schools describe their model utilizes three forms:

- the vision
- the mission
- and a longer narrative, which may include historical information

Your VISION statement should:

- be short and memorable – so that it can be memorized and repeated
- define your primary goal
- define a specific timeline
- be oriented towards the future and how you see children growing and evolving
- create a sense of stability in the long term
- be general enough to include all of your and your students' interests
- and be motivating

Your MISSION statement should answer questions such as:

- what you will do – the purpose of your school
- what you will be doing – how you'll achieve your mission
- who you serve – the kind of students you'll serve
- what value you will bring – the benefits you'll offer students

I always recommend that clients take a look at other schools' vision and mission statements to get ideas and to see how the statements are crafted. If you do a bit of research, you'll likely find that some of the newer alternative schools and micro-schools are foregoing the traditional mission and vision statements and use briefer action statements. Some schools have even chosen to re-envision the traditional statements in favor of describing their approach or philosophy to education.

Regardless of how you define your stance and what your school will do with kids, you will want to have some statements written out. I encourage you to allow them to evolve as you work through the remaining chapters.

Here are some example statements from some new and notable alternatives, as well as their websites, to allow you to be inspired!

- Alt School: Our mission is to enable all children to reach their potential. https://www.altschool.com

- Acton Academy: The Acton Academy's mission is to inspire each child and parent who enters our doors to find a calling that will change the world. https://www.actonacademy.org

- Bloom Community School: Our mission is to cultivate joyful, independent learners in an educational environment that nurtures individual development by integrating high academic standards and community engagement. https://www.bloomcommunityschool.org

- Long-View Micro-school: We focus on long-term, transferable skills and they all add up to a love of learning. http://www.long-view.com

Check out each of these micro-schools, as well as doing some research of your own. Read the longer statements about how the schools function and operate. Take notes on ideas that resonate with you, and create your own statements as you go along.

Ideal Student

Now that you have some introductory statements to inspire your school planning, your vision, your mission, and perhaps some additional narrative, it's time to define your student population. Who is your ideal client – your ideal student?

Each micro-school functions to serve a different kind of student. Whom will your school serve? Gifted students? Students with interests in particular subject areas such as mathematics and science, the arts and humanities, entrepreneurial skills, technology, or spirituality? What kind of diversity would you like to encourage? Are your ideal students multiethnic, from nuclear families or single-parent homes? Do your ideal students have special needs such as: social or emotional sensitivity, developmental delays, learning deficits, behavioral issues, or some spiritual challenges?

Go back to the meditation we did in earlier in the book and use what you learned to describe your child in detail. Give the child a name, age, and write about all of the characteristics you can remember. You may not share this information with anyone else, but keep the description of your "ideal student" with you as you begin to build your plan.

Ideal Parent

What kind of parent are you aiming to serve with your micro-school? Are you interested in meeting the needs of your local community? Are you part of a rich network of parents that you can already envision serving with your school? Are your parents working in day jobs or for themselves? Do your parents have skill sets similar to yours? How affluent are your ideal parents and what is their ability to pay tuition? Do you envision your parents offering time and effort to offset tuition costs, or would you like for them to pay for tuition in full?

Take some time to really sit with this. Parents are a key to making your micro-school work. Great parents will add to the uniqueness of your school, challenging parents will create a drain on your time and energy. Make a decision up front about what kinds of parents you want to attract to your micro-school. Just as you did with the ideal child, write up a description of your "ideal parent" to guide you as you continue to expand the plan for your micro-school.

Setting the Intention

As you continue to move forward with your micro-school building plan, you are bound to get excited. You will naturally want to talk with other adults about your vision and ideas. Now is the time to create a firm vision and to craft the language you'll use to talk with others about your micro-school.

Shared visions are a wonderful thing. If you want to partner with a few other parents at this stage of the game, you can tackle this portion of the work together. Just know that holding firm to a vision and mission becomes increasingly difficult as you add more ideas to the formulation stages. Just as the old saying goes, too many cooks can spoil the broth. With too many inputs, you may find yourself with tons of ideas and little clarity. So set your intention with a clear vision and mission for your micro-school and the way forward will be easier.

Chapter 6

Building Block #4 – Location, Location, Location

A child's geographic location, race, or parent's income
level should not predetermine their life's course and it's
up to us to see that they don't.

- Joe Manchin

Now that we've looked at your plan, the legalities, and
your special sauce, it's time to tackle the location of
your school. I began this chapter with West Virginia
Governor Joe Manchin's quote because I think it
speaks to the importance of location upon our lives.

No matter where our students come from or what situations they find themselves being raised in, schools have
the potential to offer something different, something up-
lifting. The space that we provide our students to learn
in has a profound influence on the learning process. A

school and its learning spaces can either inspire and uplift students or it can send subtle messages about power and control. While students may have little control over the physical surroundings that make up their home environment, you can offer the very best environments to support learning on the part of your students.

As the old real estate saying goes, there are three important considerations when it comes to purchasing a property: location, location, location.

Let's talk a little bit about your school's physical environment. Physical aspects of structure and layout are critical variables that affect a student's attitude towards learning. A student's involvement in creating the learning environment can either empower them or reduce their participation and motivation for learning. There are several research projects underway to examine the impact that a school's physical environment has upon student engagement, enjoyment, and achievement.

Many school in the US, as well as schools globally, suffer from disrepair, due to shrinking budgets. Today, the greatest proportion of money in a school's budget is spent on staff salaries and benefits, or on materials versus on creating a pleasing atmosphere for students. Building maintenance or remodeling are often not an option when budgets dwindle. So what do we already know about the impact poor physical environments have upon students?

Often referred to as "cells and bells," most traditional public schools were created with small "cell-like" classrooms, with a system of "bells" to tell students when to get up and move to the next room. The model has been around for over a century and is rooted in the industrial revolution. It does not match the current trend to offer students a more personalized, student-centered learning experience. And, although architecture isn't the single problem in today's schools, it can contribute significantly to a student's learning experience.

Where new building or remodeling is taking place, some principles of design have emerged. There are particular elements which appear to positively influence both student attitude and achievement. Here is a list of some of the best new options for student learning spaces:

- modular seating options – think modular couches, the kind of furniture that students can rearrange to suit their individual and group needs
- soft cushions and pillows – an antidote to the stiff wooden chairs seen in many classrooms
- moveable walls or cubicles – allowing students to create smaller areas for individual work when quiet is needed
- bright natural lighting – versus overhead fluorescent lighting so many traditional schools use as a cost saving measure
- green spaces – outdoor classroom areas to work hands on with living materials as well as to learn and relax in natural settings

There are many reasons for taking a long look at the learning space you'll use as your micro-school. There is some preliminary evidence that aesthetically pleasing classrooms actually promote higher levels of achievement. For our purposes however, you may just want to focus on the fact that your creation of a pleasing learning space will demonstrate your care and concern for your students. Students who are given a beautiful space to learn in feel safer and more secure. This will demonstrate to your students that they matter.

So to begin, let's consider where you might hold classes. There are several broad categories of "buildings" you will likely consider:

- using your own space
- renting/borrowing space
- purchasing space
- building space
- conducting learning outside

The first question to ask yourself about space is, what do my students truly need or want? If you did the meditation and wrote about your ideal student, then you likely have clues about space. You will have seen your student in action and know if they are the kind that prefers to be outdoors, or inside cuddled up in a pile of pillows. You'll know if your ideal student needs a quiet space to get work done, or if they prefer the high energy of sitting at a table with other kids in collaboration.

Using Your Own Space

One of the ways to get started quickly with your microschool and to save money is to use your own space. If you are a homeschooling parent, this might mean opening up your family room workspace to several other children while you seek out additional options as your school grows.

This is precisely what my friend, Marcy, did. She began by homeschooling her two daughters. When she got together with friends for playdates and the other moms found out what she was doing, most were curious. Over time, as these moms saw how happy and bright Marcy's girls were, that they were actually more precocious, a few started asking direct questions. Could Marcy teach their children as well? So she quickly added a few tables and pillows to the family room and voila, her micro-school was born!

You can do this too. Think about your own property. Do you have a barn or garage that might easily be converted into a learning space? Do you have an unused basement or family room with great lighting and lots of open space? With a few touch ups, you may well have a space to begin with a handful of students. Of course, one thing to consider with any repurposed space is access to bathroom facilities for your students. And you'll also need to consider how food will be handled.

You'll want to check your homeowner's insurance policy to make sure that repurposing your space is legal. You may have to add some additional liability insurance to your policy to bring it up to code. The added expense in repurposing your own space will be well worth the savings you reap in not needing to secure an outside location.

Renting / Borrowing Space

The next easiest way to create the space for your micro-school students to learn is to consider renting or borrowing a space in your community. This is not only a great way to expand the size and reach of your school – allowing more students to attend than you might be able to serve in your home-based location – but it also creates visibility for your school.

Some of the places that micro-schools are popping up include:

- in under-utilized storefronts in strip malls
- in church social halls, Sunday school spaces, or gymnasiums
- in community centers
- in coffee shops or co-working spaces
- and even in a portion of a local business' office space

While the first three spaces are probably familiar to you, the latter two ideas may be a bit more surprising. A few micro-schools have found their humble beginnings as meet-ups at the local coffee shop. When a few home-schooling parents get together for coffee, and the kids sit in the back room to work on their lessons, new possibilities are generated. Some micro-school planners have taken this idea a step further, opening up a coffee-shop with a large adjacent space for learning, actually recruiting students from their customer base. Micro-schools that are part of co-working spaces function much in the same way. As entrepreneurs join the co-working space and begin to have families, the offerings for child care and tutoring services within the site can be expanded into full-blown micro-school offerings.

One of the newest micro-school ideas is a "school-with-in-a-business." Partly inspired by Apple's "Alt-School" micro-school initiative, some small business owners are considering expanding their onsite day-care options to allow employees' children to be nearby at all times. In the case where a business is interested in internships, the micro-school can actually blur lines between a student's studies and opportunities to learn "on the job" alongside parents. This is truly a modern-day nod to the apprenticeship model of yesteryear.

Purchasing Space(s)

Eventually most micro-school builders consider purchasing a space of their own. As enrollment swells and space gets tight, there is a need for expansion. Sometimes this includes securing space to ease overcrowding, and sometimes it's a function of creating a satellite location that's near some particular attraction or opportunity for expanded learning.

Whatever your reason for considering the purchase of a space for your micro-school, you'll need to think ahead. While there are some great stories out there about alternative and micro-school builders securing donations of land or buildings, there is the inevitable consideration of funds. We'll touch on aspects of funding in the next chapter, where you'll find lots of ideas about how to generate additional revenue for your school, including capital campaigns for the purchase of buildings.

Building Space

Very similar to purchasing a space for your school, building a space is a real possibility for today's micro-school founder. But it's not something I recommend you do out of the gate, with all of the other responsibilities you'll have in setting up your school.

One of the cool things that's happening with micro-schools that decide to build is the involvement of students in all aspects of the work. Students in your micro-school can and should be part of that visioning process. Many micro-school builders are actually creating curriculum around the architectural design of their proposed building, incorporating content area instruction in math, physics, and environmental science into the process.

Kids who help to design their building become highly engaged in learning. And the process doesn't stop with design. There are opportunities for kids to meet with architects in person, and to get their hands dirty with some of the physical building aspects of the project. Advertising a capital fundraising campaign, and learning to work directly with potential donors, is another area kids can be involved with. Letter writing, done by kids on behalf of their school, is a very effective way to secure funding from key donors for all sorts of fundraising efforts. This kind of authentic learning opportunity gets students involved, as well as providing real-world experience in writing for a purpose.

When thinking about building physical spaces for your school I recommend "envisioning the castle but starting with the cottage." That is – dream big. Involve your families and students in a planning process that includes many buildings, or a campus environment. Then work backwards and choose to begin with the building that has the most functional aspects. Build that structure first and then add on to your plan over the years as your school settles into its full life cycle. There will be plenty of time to continue the building process over time with each new batch of students who join your micro-school.

Conducting Learning Outdoors

There is a new form of micro-school gaining popularity across the globe – providing kids an opportunity to do all of their learning outside in nature. Sometimes referred to as "outdoor learning" or "learning in nature," there is a new idea you'll find if you search online for "forest schools." These micro-schools utilize the environment as the main catalyst for teaching and learning. Forest schools provide students with both pedagogy (the methods by which to learn) as well as a physical space (the environment for learning).

These unique schools don't have to be created in wooded areas only. As a micro-school builder, you can consider the various outdoor spaces available to you as a natural extension to the indoor classroom environment. Outdoor learning is great for building independence and self-esteem in students. And the fact that learning in nature is cross-curricular is powerful. Students who are learning outside can dig in deeply on topics such as: the role of trees in an ecosystem, or plant and animal recognition, and biology. Outdoor spaces are also great for learning mathematical concepts and communication in new and exciting ways.

Hours of Operation

In a similar vein to location, you'll want to consider the hours of operation for your micro-school. Depending on your space, hours of operation can be dependent on several factors. If you are operating a school which functions mainly outdoors, in general you'll want your students to attend during daylight. In areas where extreme temperature fluctuations occur, timing of your micro-school day will also be critical.

Hours of operation are one of those things we tend to lump into a "this is what we always do" sort of box. In the case of traditional schools, it's most common to see the older students heading off to school in the wee hours of the morning, with younger students following along shortly afterwards. Most often in public schools, hours of operation have more to do with the ability to bus the student population to and from school safely, with the available transportation.

Because most micro-schools function around parents providing transportation, it's great to take parents' needs and wants into consideration when laying out your hours of operation. This is one of those places where you can get creative. If the bulk of your students are "middle-schoolers" you might consider starting later and ending later, to accommodate the shifts in their hormones, which often causes them to stay up later and sleep in later. There are real biological mechanisms at play here, and with some flexible scheduling at your micro-school, you can engage your students in learning at the times most beneficial to them vs. when it suits your schedule.

Inviting Potential Families

One of the most powerful things that will happen when you settle on a location is the ability to invite families to events on the property you've chosen for your micro-school. After completing your business plan, you will need to begin to recruit potential partners, families, and students. Once you've chosen the space where you'll open your micro-school, you can invite each of these sets of stakeholders to participate in mock lessons or activities. Holding informational meetings and planning sessions in your space gives potential partners and clients a chance to get a feeling of what the micro-school will actually feel like.

As you now realize, your micro-school's location will cost money. Whether it's in upgrading an existing space you own, or renting, buying or building a space, the physical environment you use for your micro-school will necessitate the generation of capital of some sort. So the next logical step in the micro-school building process is to tackle the issue of money.

Chapter 7

Building Block #5 – Show Me the Money!

Making money is art and working is art
and good business is the best art.

- Andy Warhol

I think I can hear you again. Was that you screaming in pain as you turned the page and found out we were going to be talking about money? And was that you thinking, rats … I just want to work with the kids!

If you have some anxiety or fear around money, you are not alone. It's important, though, to face this fear as the visionary and owner/operator of a micro-school. You don't absolutely have to tend to the finances yourself – it's easy enough to outsource bookkeeping and tax services – however you do need to have a basic understanding of how the money flows in and out of your micro-school.

In this chapter, we are going to take a look at all of the financial aspects you'll need to address in building your micro-school. We'll take a bit of a "top down" approach – beginning with the high level costs that are related to the micro-school itself and then end the chapter with a look at how your personal financial situation will impact the process.

An Overall Micro-School Budget (Expenses)

To get you warmed up, let's look at the big "line items" you'll likely include in your micro-school budget. Setting up a budget now, will not only keep you on target in terms of fundraising to get your school off the ground, it will help to keep you accountable for spending aligned to the money you have on hand.

A typical school has a business manager to do this sort of work. You'll want to put on that hat for a moment, even if you plan to outsource the work, so that you understand all of the ways in which you'll see money going in and out of your micro-school. Even if you plan to function as a non-profit, you'll still need to maintain budget documentation for accounting purposes.

To get some experience with budgeting, I recommend you set up a spreadsheet. You can use MS Excel, Apple's Numbers, or Sheets in Google Drive to get you going. Most of these tools have templates you can use to get a basic budget started. The typical line items you'll find in a school budget include:

- Teaching staff (full time/part time)
- Additional instructors (this includes guest mentors or speakers)

- Support staff (child care providers, monitors, and the like)
- Technicians (people who take care of your computers or network if you have them)
- Administrative and clerical staff (could be you as the owner, and a secretary or bookkeeper if you hire them)
- Caretaker/Cleaner (the folks you pay to tend your physical property)
- Building costs (rent or mortgage payments if you have them)
- Building Maintenance (costs related to keeping your building)
- Energy (electric, gas, etc. to keep the lights on and heating/cooling running)
- Insurance (property, liability, and possibly life-insurance – for you and/or staff)
- Catering (any food you provide to students or for events)
- Classroom supplies (furniture, books, computers, art supplies, etc.)
- Other resources (anything else that you need to pay for that doesn't fit the other categories)

Create columns in your spreadsheet after the budget items and include headings for:

- the total proposed budget,
- projected to date expenditures,
- actual to date expenditures,
- the variance,
- and the actual budget.

These columns will let you set the costs up front to help you keep on track, and then document expenses to make sure you don't take your micro-school into the red. As you are planning your school, it's a good idea to do some initial projections. Make a copy of your spreadsheet and begin to fill in your best guess as to what each of the line items may cost you. Set the column to do an automatic sum of the line items and you'll have a ballpark figure to use when you begin to tackle tuition and funding.

Now that you have your initial budget, take some time to think about any additional fees you haven't included on the list. Sometimes there are hidden expenses related to getting your micro-school off the ground. Are you going to purchase new computers for staff, or for students? Will you need to buy furniture such as chairs and tables, or floor pillows, and room dividers? Do you need outdoor equipment? Make a list of all of the things you want to purchase to make your school unique and enjoyable for kids and come up with a total number of what you'll need to make those purchases.

Income Sources

We've taken a look at some of the many ways that money will flow out of your micro-school. So now it's time to turn our attention to the ways you'll generate income with your micro-school. Those sources of revenue can take several forms. The most obvious form of income for a micro-school is the collection of tuition. However, there are some innovative methods you can consider, both during start-up and as you begin to run your micro-school. We'll touch on ways to do fundraising, both traditional and in more modern ways, as well as how you can solicit donations, seek grants, or consider partnerships and/or investors.

Tuition

If you do a quick search on the internet for the term "micro-school" (as I'm guessing you already have), then you'll likely know that the current description of a micro-school on Wikipedia states that micro-schools offer a full year of education for $10,000 or less. While this number is generally more than what a local school district receives from the government as reimbursement for each student, the number can be seen as arbitrary. Many of today's micro-schools seek to be more affordable than other private school options, while others situate themselves to be affordable to most families, regardless of their ability to pay.

These are all major decisions for you to make as you consider how much tuition you will charge your students. If you have no idea what you should charge, it's a good idea to do a survey of the market in your area. What does the best private school charge per year? How much does it cost to attend the local Catholic or religious school? Also ask yourself what the education you are offering is worth.

How much money did you determine you need to bring in to your school in your first attempt at a budget? How many students do you intend to take into your school? One simple way to get an idea about tuition is to divide your total budget by the number of students you'd like to enroll. Of course, tuition isn't the only mechanism for generating revenue in your school, but it's one of the largest sources. So using it as a ballpark figure isn't a bad idea.

Let's play this out in real numbers. Imagine that you intend to operate your school on a budget of $150,000 a year: $50K for your salary as the director and main teacher, $50K for additional staffing costs and $50K for all other insurance, supplies, building costs etc. Next, imagine that you'd like to keep your enrollment small, let's say 10 students to start. 150K divided across ten students is the equivalent of $15K in tuition for each of your students. Using that example, ask yourself: Is that a fee that parents in my community would pay for the kind of education I'm going to offer?

You'll also want to consider some options for in-kind donations to offset your tuition costs. Many micro-schools offer families a sliding scale based on ability to pay. Those who can afford more, pay more; those who can't, are offered a reduced tuition expense. In such cases, it's customary to ask parents at the reduced tuition rate to provide time and effort in some way, to help the school function. This can range from the offering of accounting or other professional services to actual physical labor in helping to clean the building or property, to serving as before or after care child support on a particular day of the week. Get creative here – there are many ways to make tuition flexible to meet the needs of your clients as well as your own.

I'd like to give you a thought to ponder. There is a current belief in the business world that the more we pay for something, the more we value it. While your ambitions in opening a micro-school may be noble, in helping children of any means to have access to a truly remarkable equation, you will want to balance your altruistic intent with some practical wisdom.

At least during the start-up phase of your micro-school, it may make sense to charge a larger tuition than you may feel comfortable with. You'll always have the option to do some fundraising for tuition supports for your students who can't afford to attend. What you'll gain in charging a higher rate to start is a smaller, more dedicated, and focused clientele. You'll be able to attract the client who values the kind of education you are providing and is willing to pay full price for it. This kind of parent is likely to be a strong ally, helping you to grow your micro-school and to secure additional funds more easily.

The larger your tuition payment, the fewer students you'll need to attract as clients. The fewer students you have attending your micro-school, the more personalized attention and customized learning opportunities you can offer.

In the end, the choice of what to charge for tuition is up to you.

Fundraising

Even before you launch your micro-school, it makes sense to think about and plan for fundraising. Even if your chosen tuition payments cover your projected budget for the first year, there are likely to be things pop up that require additional funds. From opportunities to take a field trip to a local event to unforeseen breakage of key equipment, there will always be a need for more funds than you have coming into your micro-school through the collection of tuition.

Fundraising can take all sorts of forms for your micro-school. There are the typical bake-sales, candy sales, and popcorn sales. Your students can create items to sell and run a maker faire, or you can upload their designs to websites that print gifts on demand with each child's artwork. You can hold fund-raising events such as car washes, theatrical or musical performances, poetry-slams, or even set up a booth at local event to gather donations.

Whatever methods you choose, be sure to involve your families in the decision-making process. Get consensus around what sorts of fundraising they'd be willing to promote, and what they'd like to raise funds for. By getting family and student buy-in before launching a fundraising event, you are much more likely to actually generate the funds you need for your micro-school.

Donations

One traditional way to raise funds is to ask for donations. Creating a reliable group of donors and a steady stream of donations can be an art. It's a powerful revenue generation machine, especially if you become a non-profit or partner with a non-profit, offering your donors a way to make tax deductible contributions to your micro-school. There are lots of benefactors out there who will find your innovative micro-school to be of interest, so make yourself a list of potential donors now and add to the list as you begin to speak about your plans. Getting them to consider making an annual "planned gift" to your micro-school through a non-profit partner is a great way to enhance your funds generation.

Be sure to do some research on when the best time to ask for donations is in your area. Sometimes it's at year end. Some localities have events around an "annual day of giving" scheduled and prompted in various media channels. This is a great way to get your micro-school's message out to a broader audience. And once you have students enrolled, incorporate students messaging donors on a regular basis as an authentic way to keep them connected, informed, and to encourage continued support.

Capital Campaigns

When it's time to make larger purchases for your micro-school, you'll want to consider a capital campaign. Capital campaigns are larger, more focused fundraising projects when you determine it's time to acquire or improve the physical assets of your micro-school. You've probably seen these sorts of campaigns displayed in local organizations with a "thermometer" type graphic to showcase progress along the way.

In order to make a capital campaign a viable option, you'll have to be clear about the purpose and time-frame. Everyone in the micro-school should be a part of the planning and agree upon the amount of funds, their purpose, and the activities you'll conduct to raise the money.

Crowdfunding

Crowdfunding is all the rage today when people want to get something started quickly with little to no money of their own. It's based on the principles of getting a large number of people to donate smaller sums of money, eventually leading to the full amount you need to launch your project. Similar to what you'll do with other fundraising events, crowdfunding will help you generate cash quickly. The main difference is that most of the work will take place on the internet.

Crowdfunding is deceptively simple to create, and much more of an art to pull off. Most first-time crowd-funders make the mistake of posting their project and then sitting back to see the funds roll in. There are some great books on Amazon debunking the myth of instant cash, and offering the support you need to craft an amazing campaign that delivers. You'll learn lots about how to prime the pumps before you start your campaign, how to message regularly to get the biggest results, and how to reward your donors in ways that get them excited to participate. And if you are really serious about making your crowdfunding campaign work, you'll want to spend time looking at other successful cam-paigns to see what they did, or even consider hiring a coach who specializes in getting campaigns funded.

There are lots of crowdfunding platforms out there to choose from. How do you know which one is best for your micro-school? Below are details about the three options I feel work best for micro-school builders. I've also shared some information about why I think one of the biggest platforms is a mistake for micro-school builders, at least at the start.

GoFundMe – www.gofundme.com

Arguably the largest crowdfunding platform, GoFundMe has helped individuals to raise over three billion in funds since its debut in 2010. The platform allows users to create a page and share their funding request out to the world through social media platforms. GoFundMe makes its money by deducting a small fee from every donation made. If a user makes no money, then no charges are incurred. GoFundMe is unique in that users do not need to offer incentives to donors and so it's often the site of choice for personal projects and causes. GoFundMe is an ideal platform for you to consider in the early stages of your micro-school planning process. Once you have your mission and vision set, you can set up a campaign to help you with initial start-up costs and with recruiting a core team of partners and employees.

Indiegogo – *www.indiegogo.com*

Started in 2008, Indiegogo is a crowdfunding platform designed to support the solicitation of funds for ideas, charities, or start-up businesses. This makes it an ideal platform for your micro-school, once you've convened your core team and are ready to gather the funds you need to purchase materials, pay initial salaries, or secure your location. Indegogo has looser guidelines than some of the other platforms and is particularly beneficial when it comes to the disbursement of donated fund, which happens nearly instantly.

Patreon – *www.patreon.com*

A membership platform vs. a crowdfunding platform, Patreon is a site to consider if you would like to attract ongoing donations from supporters. Based on the idea of an arts patron in the past, the site allows a donor to set up an ongoing donation towards the works you are creating. You might consider setting up an account to support your personal endeavors, or to support your work as the founder of the school during your startup phase.

Kickstarter – *www.kickstarter.com*

Kickstarter is one of the most popular crowdfunding platforms available. I chose to place it last in this list as I don't feel it's the best fit for micro-school builders for the following reasons. First, it's designed to support "creative projects." Now you might think your micro-school project is creative, and I would agree with you. But you only need to do a search of the kinds of projects being funded on Kickstarter to quickly see that very few are educational in nature, and the bulk are focused more on the traditional art forms. That's not to say you can't fund an educational project on Kickstarter – my friend Lindsey and her partners got startup funds for their curriculum project that way. However, there's another reason I don't recommend Kickstarter to my micro-school building clients. It's because of the way in which funds are gathered and distributed. With Kickstarter, you set your funding goal. If you meet or exceed your goal, your donors are billed, and you receive your funds shortly afterward. If you don't meet your funding goals, however, no funds are collected and distributed to you. In my mind, that's a huge risk to take – to spend the time and effort to plan and launch a campaign for your micro-school and to not reap the benefits of donations made. This could work to your advantage however, if you are someone that needs to have a sense of urgency to motivate your action. If that's you, and if the threat of losing all funds promised is enough to get you to step up your messaging to potential donors, then give it a go. Good luck!

Investors & Grants

As you continue to consider avenues for generating revenue to build your micro-school, you may want to consider outside investors. Most large cities now have business incubators which work to match innovators, like you, with angel donors and investors. If you are willing to share your micro-school idea with others who have the cash, then this kind of partnership from the start may be for you. You'll want to approach an incubator or investor with your vision and mission well planned out. Refer back to your notes to get yourself ready. Once you've finished the steps in this book, you can also assemble your ideas into a formal business proposal to share.

Some people think that grants are an option for microschool builders. And if you've either partnered with a non-profit 501c3 or are going to apply for the status yourself, then grants are a possibility down the road. The majority of grants available today for educational innovation of this sort, however, are aimed at increasing capacity to existing programs. Interested in seeing their funds used to expand successful programming and sharing models out more broadly, most grant makers shy away from making grants to individuals in the start-up phase of their project. Grants are a great consideration once you're up and running your micro-school, so consider putting the ideas on a back burner while you get going. There are big entities, such as Apple, who are interested in the small schools movement. Keep an eye out for ways in which you might involve yourself in their efforts and offerings, potentially speeding up your own process.

It's Mostly about You

This last part of our overview of money may come as a surprise to you. Because it's all about you. If you're a busy entrepreneur, teacher, or parent, then money will likely be a focus of your daily life. It's important to make sure that your personal finances are in order before undertaking the task of opening a micro-school. If you are in financial distress, or out of work, starting a micro-school as the answer to your prayers may seem like a good idea. However, the increased stress you'll face every day to make it work will put an unnecessary amount of stress upon your ideas and your potential collaborators.

If you're ready to go "all in," so to speak, and make a micro-school your main source of revenue, you'll fare best if you do some thinking ahead about how to make ends meet while you're locating the finances and enrolling students. Scaling back your own personal work and services is one way you can free up time and energy to put toward your micro-school planning. It's also a good idea to take inventory of the number of hours you have available each day to devote towards your micro-school planning efforts. Unless you make space and time a priority for the planning work being laid out before you, there is a high likelihood your plan will go unfinished and your school will remain just a dream.

In my case, when I decided to begin working on the micro-schools idea, I made some difficult choices about how I was living my life in order to fund my mission and movement. I sold my three-bedroom townhouse to eliminate my mortgage payment and purchased instead a 900 square foot apartment in a cooperative. My expenses in that building are incredibly low, freeing up my income to put toward building my business.

If you are a teacher who is ready to make a change, look into the option of taking an early retirement. Many times, the amount of money you are eligible to withdraw on a monthly basis is enough to cover your basic living expenses, leaving you free to draw a smaller salary from your micro-school. This frees up your funds to hire more staff, or purchase that building you're dreaming about even sooner than you initially planned.

If you are a homeowner, you can consider taking out a home equity loan to get your school started. If you're already a small business owner, you can explore a business loan as well. If you intend to borrow money to get started, however, be sure to spend more time on your budgets to ensure that the personal liability you are taking on has a proper plan for repayment.

Finally, one of the most important things you'll want to do, related to the money you need for your micro-school, is to adopt a positive money mindset. The way in which you think about money has a direct impact upon how things turn out. Do you have friends who are always complaining about being poor or about not having enough money to make ends meet? Have you ever noticed how they never seem able to get a leg up and turn the corner related to finances? Much of their problem stems from mindset.

The opposite is true. Do you have friends who celebrate the abundance in their lives, reveling in the simple things they have? Do you notice how they don't need much to make themselves happy, and yet always seem to have more than enough to share with others? The same will hold true for your micro-school. Adopt an attitude that the funds you need to start are waiting to find you and you're bound to start off on the right foot!

Chapter 8

Building Block #6 – David vs. Goliath
(or, Slaying the Dreaded Curriculum)

In America, we have 19th century school conditions
and a curriculum that prepares our kids for the 1990s.

- Heidi Hayes Jacobs

If you've ever been to a meeting at your child's school,
you've likely heard the term "curriculum" used often.
Perhaps you've been told, "The curriculum we follow
doesn't allow us to XYZ." Or you might have heard,
"Your daughter is performing well below her grade level
and the pace of the curriculum is increasing the gap further."

While the classical definition of curriculum includes all
of the experiences a student has while learning, the
term more commonly refers to a planned sequence of
instruction – or looking at a student's learning in terms
of their progress in meeting instructional goals.

I'd like to ask you to sit with that for just a moment. If you are reading this book, if you've already done the hard work of finding your child a learning environment that inspires her, or have gotten him out of one that was crushing his spirit – then you may be taken aback with the notion of curriculum.

Its time I come totally clean with you – for most of my adult life, I was a public school teacher who not only utilized curriculum, but also believed whole-heartedly in the need for curriculum to ensure every child had an equal chance to succeed. Now that I am an independent consultant, no longer required to follow curriculum when I work with children, I realize the folly in that notion of curriculum.

I think that many of you will agree with me that curriculum, on the surface, sounds great. Create a pathway for learning that ensures important content is taught to students.

But how do we decide what content is worth teaching, and who do we allow to champion that cause?

In this day and age, it's nearly impossible to point to a single person who guides the creation of standards, curriculum, the textbooks that offer content, or the assessments that check to see if students have memorized the ideas. The big system of education is a behemoth, faceless and nameless. One might argue that at least in the US, the Secretary of Education is the person responsible, but just looking at the current appointee to that office (in 2018, it's Betsy DeVos, heiress to the Proctor and Gamble fortunes) and one must wonder who is really steering the boat, and what their goals actually are.

This discussion could easily derail our work so far.... So many who seek to make change get bogged down in trying to reform a system vs. taking small, personal, and actionable steps.

I've come to the realization that there is no real way for individuals to change the big system of education, and there is no good reason to try to do so. I've come to the realization that real change happens in small ways, slowly and quietly, with small groups of caring people. Innovation doesn't happen out in the bright lights on the stage – it happens in the quiet moments after midnight as a thoughtful person works and reworks an idea until it shines.

I believe that you and I are those sorts of innovators. I believe that you and I are like David from the bible, standing up to face a Goliath (curriculum). And like David, our courage, and our tiny innovations (our micro-schools) will eventually slay the giant of curriculum. I believe that you and I will make real change by taking the learning out of the hands of adults and returning it where it always belonged – back into the hands of the students.

Self-Directed Learning

If the topic of learner-centered schools or self-directed learning is of interest to you, I can recommend some of the visionaries who have published on the theme. If you want to know about the ways in which school kills children's creativity, you'll enjoy the writings and TED Talks of Sir Ken Robinson. If you want to know more about children building their knowledge through doing things with their hands, then read the works of John Dewey and about the constructivist movement. If you want to learn more about parents taking responsibility for their children's learning, then you can't do better than reading the writings of John Holt. If you want know how someone takes a thought and turns it into a school, read the writings of A.S. Neil, about how he created Summerhill. Certainly, there are a LOT more great authors out there to read. A search will turn up all sorts of stories of innovators starting small schools, and stories about brave parents taking action on behalf of their children.

Self-directed, learner-centered education, I believe, is the future we must all want for our children. The world is changing so rapidly, it no longer makes sense to teach concrete sets of knowledge to everyone, unless a child senses that he or she is meant to work in a particular field. Our single biggest gift to today's children, especially at a young age, is to instill a passion for learning, to cultivate the child's curiosity. Our world needs citizens who are capable of learning and growing throughout a lifetime, regardless of whether they are enrolled in formal education.

So how can you tackle the issue of curriculum in your micro-school? How can you situate school so that children have the freedom to learn in their own way? How can you offer something that so few other schools offer, and find families who are willing to do things differently with you?

If you are thinking about starting your micro-school with the youngest children, starting with pre-schoolers and adding on "grade-levels" as each year passes, you'll have an easier time starting with learner-centered education. You'll be able to build self-directed learning processes as you go, then allowing those frameworks to guide children as they mature. If, however, you are interested in working with older children, there may be a bit of "deprogramming" you will need to do first, in order to help them fully embrace the freedom of self-directed learning.

Making the Transition

One of the things that may happen as you begin to seek out students to attend your micro-school is a feeling of resistance from some parents to their child going from the structure of public school to the freedoms your micro-school offers. No matter what stance you take with your special sauce, your offerings are likely to feel quite different from what most parents and kids know as the norm, when it comes to school. So how do you address the disconnect?

First, you'll want to talk gently with parents about how kids really learn. You might want to locate some adults in your proximity who have grown up as homeschoolers or in an alternative education setting and who can speak to its power. Meeting adults who have been homeschooled, or alternatively educated, and who "haven't been ruined" is a great way to help prospective parents and students see the power of learning without so many structures in place.

Next, you may actually want to consider creating a scaffolded approach for your older enrollees. That is, you may want to build in mechanisms that allow kids to decompress and adjust to freedom found in your micro-school gradually. There are several ways you can do this.

At Summerhill, they actually allow new students to do nothing all day, for as long as it takes, until the student becomes bored and begins to look at what other students are doing with curiosity. It's important to note that Summerhill has a policy to not take students over the age of 11. Their rationale is that, beyond that age, most students are unable to make the transition to self-directed learning successfully.

So if you want to take middle or high school students into your micro-school who have spent some time in traditional educational settings, you may want to offer an alternative to help students transition. Some micro-school builders ease the discomfort by having their older enrollees initially register as cyber students. Because the student will continue to follow a more traditional curricular path, one that they are familiar with, while being given the opportunity to have more freedom to decide when, where, and how they will tackle the learning content, many find the transition to independent learning easier.

I like to call the process of using outside curriculum or a cyber-enrollment as an option for learners as the "double-dip." By allowing your students to transition out of a traditional public or private school setting by using more familiar curricular structures, your students can begin to "taste-test" the freedoms offered by learner-centered alternatives. Hopefully, once the transition is complete, your students will come to love to learn in their own, self-directed ways.

Building Learner-Centered "Curriculum"

Part of what makes micro-schools so powerful is that they sit outside of the big system of education and the confines of standards, curriculum, and assessment. They are more agile, and better equipped to meet the needs of each child as an individual. What they can do, which larger schools struggle to do, is to address the broader classical definition of what curriculum is intended to do. That is, micro-schools can guide the totality of student experiences that occur, as part of the documented educational process.

As you build your school, you will need to find a way to facilitate this more natural learning process. One quick and efficient way to get started is to utilize the services of others who have tackled the issue of learner-centered content for you. There are providers who offer static "lessons" you can use to guide students' explorations, while others offer the whole package, and include the support of teachers to monitor students' progress and to facilitate dialogue when needed.

Several to check out to get you started are:

- Global Village School: www.globalvillageschool.org. They offer accredited and customizable curriculum, designed for homeschooling families but also applicable for your setting.
- Laurel Springs School www.laurelsprings.com. A private, accredited, and online K-12 education provider.
- Oak Meadow. www.oakmeadow.com. A publisher of homeschool curricular materials who also offers an accredited online school.

You'll want to keep your eyes out for new and upcoming services. For instance, I was recently introduced to an amazing group of young educators whose mission is to deliver affordable, high quality, online classes. Their responsiveness to student interests means that, as a partner in your educational offerings, students will have a say in what they learn and how they learn it.

Hiring Alternatively Trained Educators

In the next chapter, we will talk about human resources for your schools – all of the people you will want to recruit to be part of your micro-school. One of the categories of people you'll need to consider are "teachers." I put the term in quotes because there is much dialogue about what a teacher is, what the function of a teacher should be, and whether or not today's children actually need to be taught at all. In the case of your micro-school, you'll want to consider whether or not to employ teachers, and what characteristics they might need to demonstrate to satisfy your learning model.

There are a number of teacher preparation programs globally which prepare "teachers" to work with students in the ways we have been discussing. If you are considering hiring teachers for your micro-school, you might look into those programs to find potential candidates. Alternative preparation for educators is beginning to happen in places such as Goddard and Marlboro Colleges in Vermont, and at Antioch University in California.

Flipping Your "Curriculum"

In traditional educational settings, there is a new method of learning called "the flipped classroom." In a nutshell, the teacher assigns online or video-based learning content as students' homework, allowing class time to be spent directly working on problems with expert guidance. The wisdom here is that when students make mistakes, the teacher is immediately aware, helping the student to correct and understand the mistakes, allowing errors to be utilized to deepen understanding. When students take practice work home as homework, mistakes often turn into patterned thinking, which can take longer to undo on the part of the teacher. Flipping curriculum can encourage students to use mistakes positively, as a learning opportunity.

The one thing to note about the innovative idea of "flipping the classroom" is that the methods still are in service to covering required content as the most important thing, versus the student and his interest and passions as central to the purpose of learning. So what I recommend is that you borrow the methods, and then apply them to a student generated "curriculum" map.

In order to offer students an opportunity to truly learn from the place of their interests and passions, you'll want to set up a process by which your students map out a plan of learning for a particular timeframe. This might be a week, a month, a semester, or even the full year. Many who use this strategy of mapping out learning begin by looking at the state or national standards for each student's particular age and/or grade-level. These are used as conversation starters about "what students your age might be expected to master in a year." Students engaged in thinking about what their peers are being expected to master will often come up with incredible ideas about how the same learning can be done in a more creative and independent fashion. Working from the standards also allows for each child to have a differentiated learning experience that has just enough difficulty to help him grow, vs. becoming bored or frustrated with material that is either too easy or too difficult.

When it comes to designing student-centered learning plans, you'll also need to consider assessments. One way to demonstrate mastery of independently curated content is to have students document their learning process. This method is borrowed from the home-schooling movement, where families are required to keep a learning portfolio to submit to the local school district as evidence for review once a year.

If the idea of keeping student portfolios appeals to you, there are lots of ways to approach the task. Begin by contacting some local districts to gather information about how they approach the task. Look at their re-quirements and think about how you can set up a sys-tem in your micro-school to document evidence that matches the learning outcomes required for children of various ages. Students can be part of this process, set-ting up a three-ring binder, or, if they are older, by creat-ing a digital portfolio to gather, showcase, and reflect upon learning that has taken place.

In public and private schools, students with identified special needs are diagnosed and offered an Individual Educational Plan, an IEP. Your micro-school can utilize this same sort of methodology to approach the defini-tion of each student's strengths and weaknesses, a plan of action for learning, and a process of document-ing the growth. At the end of each year, you'll take time with the student and their family to review the progress and make suggestion for changes to the plan for the coming year.

Another way to have students show evidence of their learning is by creating a learning showcase. A showcase is an event, not unlike a science fair, where your students will gather to share what they have learned with the community. What differs in a showcase is that the community at large, and experts, are invited to participate as well. Students engage with adults, sharing their learning, exploring questions together, reflecting upon how they might have done things differently. In the end, the student takes time to reflect upon the process and product on his or her own, and with their teacher, mentor, or learning facilitator. Grades are generally not assigned, but rather tools such as rubrics are used to indicate areas of excellence and areas for improvement.

Rubrics are an ancient term, which, used in education, describe a set of guidelines used to evaluate the outcome of a student's learning. Rubrics generally offer a scale and points to allow a viewer to indicate particular levels of achievement on the part of the learner. They often are displayed as a table and can be used by either learners or viewers to evaluate work. Rubrics are usually offered to students prior to the start of a project to indicate expectations and to encourage the highest level of attention on the part of the student.

Rubrics are one of the tools you may choose to utilize in your micro-school to motivate student learning, as well as to communicate effectively about learning outcomes. You can find hundreds of examples of rubrics on the internet, as well as some free tools for creating them for your students.

No Limits

To wrap up this chapter, I'd like to tell you a story about my friend, Sam. I met him in the spring of 2016 in an online forum. After talking for a few weeks about the big system of education and the need for real change, we decided to meet in person to continue the conversation.

Sam had been born and raised in India. He was the product of the Indian educational system, but not in ways that most of us think of when we picture his homeland. Sam was the product of an innovative high school initiative. Founded by an educational reformer, who had the support of both Mahatma Gandhi and Prime Minister Nehru, the school operated on the premise that students who were offered the opportunity to learn without limits would exceed any expectations that might be set for them.

In listening to Sam talk about his learning as a young boy, I was stunned. When he and his classmates had an inspiration to build a nuclear-powered rocket ship, his teachers and the director of the school went to work making the idea a possibility. Over the course of three years or so, Sam and his classmates dug into the problem, with the help of their teachers, to determine the knowledge they'd need to have in order to solve their problem. They dove into studies of mathematics, physics, calculus, and space – because they had real purpose and drive to make their rocket vision a reality.

From what I can gather, Sam and his classmates never actually launched that rocket. But what I can tell you is that the preparations he went through have a lot to do with the man he is today. As an immigrant to the US as a teenager, he knew the value of education and quickly got himself several degrees in computer engineering. But unlike so many other students, Sam didn't just go to work for an employer, he started building his own business. Today, he is semi-retired, having sold several of his companies over the years. Now he devotes his time to putting his earnings to good use, looking for ways to change the educational systems in the United States, in order to impact education globally.

I see you and I as versions of Sam. Although we may not have had a chance to learn the way he did, we recognize the power of learner-centered education. Although we may have struggled to hold onto our passion and personal power while learning in ways that felt alien to our natural curiosity, we have found our way forward as adults into professions where we have some freedom to make change and to learn and grow. I see you and I as Sam's partners on this road to building micro-schools for today's creative kids. I'm so glad you are along for this amazing ride!

Chapter 9

Building Block #7 – People, People, People

Surround yourself with the dreamers and the doers, the
believers and thinkers, but most of all, surround yourself with those who see the greatness within you,
even when you don't see it yourself.

— Edmund Lee

I love this quote from Edmund Lee. It points to the kinds
of kids who may benefit the most from the creation of
your micro-school. But it also speaks to the importance
of remembering to continue to see the greatness inside
of you – to connect to your inner child – to nurture the
spark that is motivating you to do something bold.
Building a micro-school will be an adventure for sure,

and you'll want to gather the very best companions for your journey. So let's dig into the topic of people: those individuals you'll begin to look for and to recruit, to be part of your micro-school building process.

A Service Organization

In today's work world, businesses generally fall into two categories: as providing either goods or services. Schools in general fall into the category of service organizations. Taking some time to think about this, and what service means to you, will help you to settle in to the kinds of people you'd like to recruit or hire as your employees.

Your micro-school likely has a clear focus at this point, and in striving to maintain that vision, you'll need to surround yourself with like-minded people – others with the same sort of servant's heart you possess.

You as the Vision Keeper

The most important role you must take on as the creator of your micro-school is as "vision keeper." So many great ideas are born from the vision and dreams of a single person, and yet they rarely are brought fully into reality without the help of others. None of the great achievements we can see in our three-dimensional physical world can be claimed to have been the achievement of a single human visionary alone. And yet, without the guidance of the vision keeper – be it by her writings left behind, or his direct oversight during creation phases – a vision cannot happen.

At this point, you've likely thought about the roles you'll take at your micro-school. If you have been a teacher in the past, perhaps you will situate yourself as the main teacher of the school. Depending on how you plan for your students to learn, you may see yourself more as the "chief learner" or the "guide on the ride." If you have never taught children directly, or have any qualms about your ability to direct children's learning, then perhaps you will set yourself as the director, owner, or protector of the school. Perhaps you will serve multiple roles, creating meals for the students, tending to injuries or illnesses, keeping the school site clean, tending to hiring and bookkeeping, and so on. Awareness of all of the roles adults fill on a daily basis in a school is an important part in defining the roles that individuals will take in your micro-school. Next, we will take a look at some of those roles and their characteristics.

On Hiring Staff

Even if you intend to be a solo-entrepreneur at the beginning, it's likely that you will eventually need to consider hiring additional staff. We'll take a look at those roles and responsibilities in a moment, but first I'd like to tell you a story about working as the "jack-of-all-trades."

When I accepted the position as the teacher in the island schoolhouse on Matinicus, I was expected to fulfill the roles of: principal, counselor, food-service and preparation worker, and nurse. As the main educator, I taught all of my students' subjects, including: reading, mathematics, science, social studies, art, music, and health and physical education.

In my prior life as an elementary educator, I had only been responsible for teaching one or two subject areas

– and I had colleagues who were in the roles of principal, counselor, nurse and food service worker.

On Matinicus, I had my superintendent to rely upon when it came to difficult decisions, and I had access to a special education consultant when it came to the learning challenges some of my students faced. A few weeks into school, an educational aide was hired to directly support one student with a profound learning need. But for the most part, day in and day out, the primary goal of guiding students' learning sat squarely on my shoulders.

What I can tell you is that being primarily responsible for everything that went on in the one-room-schoolhouse was an awesomely exciting AND an unbelievably challenging task all wrapped up in to one. The highs were incredibly high … walking the craggy island seashore with my students searching for ocean creatures on beautiful sunny fall afternoons. And the lows were incredibly low … being fogged in on the weekend with nothing to do, nowhere to go, and no companion to talk with about the challenges. In your case, you'll likely be far less isolated than I was. And you'll have the ability to reach out and get the help you need when things get tough. (Because the island was SO small, I couldn't talk about my students with any of the island residents.)

As I shared before, I stayed on the island for about three months. I went into the job sensing that I wasn't cut out for island life full-time and quickly realized that the weather, remoteness, and my inability to get off the island some weekends to break up the monotony of the intense quiet, were making me increasingly anxious and nervous. Hearing stories about being snowed in on

139

the island for a month, I was concerned about my own ability to cope with winter.

The intensity of the responsibility of running the school under these conditions was something I came to recognize I wasn't fully prepared for, especially considering the age of my young students and their intense learning needs.

The main reason I share this story with you is to encourage you to open your micro-school with like-minded individuals – even if it's with just one other adult.

Even if you think you can do it on your own, you'll benefit from the companionship you get from having colleagues. Even if you lack the funds to pay for employees to share the tasks, it's worth it to find someone who you can barter with, or who will volunteer their time, at least to start. Even if you aren't in a remote location like I was, you'll want and need to have places to go and let off steam at the end of the day – where you can talk without divulging the personal challenges of your students to people who know them well. And you'll want to have someone close to talk to about your experiences, someone who can listen to your struggles and provide you a caring shoulder to lean on.

So who are some of the allies you'll need to consider hiring as you build your micro-school plan?

Child Care

Like it or not, a big part of what schools actually do is provide parents with child care during the day time, allowing them to work. Many parents rely upon their child's school to also provide care before and after school hours as well. You'll want to consider offering before and after-care options for your micro-school families for this same reason.

Thinking through whom you want to be responsible for this task is important. They will need to be caring adults who have gotten all of their clearances, as well as having some experience with supporting kids during these down times. If you intend to have your students complete homework, your childcare staff may want to help students tackle those items prior to arriving home, as parents who need childcare supports are often too tired to help with homework in the evening.

Food Service

Your students are likely going to be with you for seven to eight hours a day. We'll talk more about scheduling trends and opportunities in the next chapter when we tackle the creation of your business plan. The reason I mention it, though, is because it's likely that your students will need to take in some form of nourishment during their time at your micro-school.

Begin by thinking through whether or not you'll ask students to pack a lunch and snacks, whether you'll offer to feed your students, or whether your students will be learning to cook to feed themselves while attending your micro-school. In the case of the last two options, you'll need to have a staff person to either cook for or with your students. This might be you, if it's a strong interest and passion, or it might be an outside employee. You can also look to a parent who operates a local restaurant or coffee shop for support here as well.

Some micro-schools, depending on their location and vision/mission, actually make going out for lunch a part of the school day. The thinking is, that the students are going to be working as business people in the future, and that the training involved in helping students to broaden their palates and learn the etiquette of dining out, is part of what students need to learn.

I have friends who opened a charter school in my hometown in the heart of the business district. They hired a professional chef to cook the school lunches, which included many of the kinds of foods students would be offered as adults in business lunches and dinners. Over time, students began to learn to eat a wider variety of foods, and to recognize the names and ingredients found in some upscale types of dishes. The goal of the founders in all of this was to help inner-city kids get a leg up professionally.

If you do go the route of preparing meals with or for your students, you'll need to look into the legal requirements for keeping a kitchen of this sort. You may need to apply for a commercial license. If so, you'll also need to be prepared for the annual inspections from the department of health in your locality.

No matter whom you choose to handle food service work for your micro-school, be sure to think about food choice as part of students' learning. Consider maintaining a school garden to help kids learn about healthy eating options. And don't forget to do your homework on food allergies and how to handle them for each student.

Building Maintenance

No matter where you choose to house your micro-school, you will need to consider the regular maintenance of the location. If you are utilizing your own property, then the role of building maintenance may well fall upon your shoulders. If you choose to rent or buy a space, then you may consider hiring staff to perform maintenance tasks for you.

In Japan, it's not uncommon for students to be responsible for cleaning up their classroom as part of their responsibilities as learners. This is something you might want to consider in your micro-school.

When I was working in the island schoolhouse, my students would stop their work day about ten minutes before their parents arrived and sweep up the classroom. This activity served several functions. The students not only took more accountability for keeping their school need and tidy, it also helped them develop a sense of pride in their workspace. It certainly helped me out a lot, and made it much easier for the island neighbor who volunteered to come in each Sunday and wipe all the tables and mop the floor in our absence.

Bookkeeping and Accounting

As you now realize, in building a micro-school, you will be taking on the responsibility of a business owner. Keeping excellent financial records for your micro-school is a must.

In the previous chapter on money, you created an initial spreadsheet to consider your costs related to tuition in order to get a sense of what kinds of revenue you'd need to generate to run your school. And you also considered whether you will function as a non-profit or for-profit entity. In both cases, you'll need to keep excellent financial records for both tax and audit purposes. The initial budget you created is a good place to start in building up your financial documentation.

If you feel less confident about the bookkeeping and accounting process you'll need in running your school, then you'll want to consider hiring or working with financially trained professionals. Roles to consider include a bookkeeper, for the day to day documentation of income and expenses. You may also want to hire or barter for accounting services from a CPA. In my own case, for my professional business work as a sole proprietor, I maintain the bookkeeping on my own and contract with a Certified Public Accountant to discuss business decisions as well as my tax preparation.

Legal Service

Early on in this process, we looked at the legal statutes which govern the type of micro-school you can build in your state, province, or country. With that in mind, there are a number of times when securing legal support for your school will be needed. Once you have completed your business plan, you may want to have a lawyer who is familiar with school law review it for accuracy and compliance.

As you begin to set up your micro-school as a non-profit or for-profit, again, you would do well to seek out legal counsel in completing the proper applications and filings. Finally, as you take students on board, you will likely want to have legal counsel review your contracts, applications, policies, and documents. Making sure that you and your families are well protected ahead of time will alleviate the need to seek out legal representation due to a lawsuit. Suffice it to say, should that occur, you'll be grateful to have already cultivated a relationship with your legal team and to have them representing you in any proceedings that occur.

Teachers?

I've intentionally put a question mark at the end of the heading to this section. As you've now likely recognized, I have a particular feeling about the hiring of teachers as staff for your micro-school. I'll share a bit more about that, as well as some details of my story, to further explain my current opinions and stance.

When I took the position as the teacher on the island in Maine, it had been nearly ten years since I had been responsible for running a classroom for young children. My ideas about how children learn best and about how best to serve their innate capacities and curiosity had shifted dramatically in those years. As a teacher, I had learned about constructivism, project-based learning, inquiry methods, and so on – but I had never really made the connections in how to utilize those methods in my own classroom.

For several years, I was fortunate to actually DO inquiry-based learning activities with some teachers I was serving in a federal grant project around technology and the arts. Leading this kind of learning for adults helped me to understand the power of the methods in practice.

What I can tell you is this: Many teachers were unable to grasp the concepts of student-centered learning, even with four years of opportunity to learn about and practice them. My sense of why that occurred was simply that, because they had never been offered an opportunity to do inquiry as students, many teachers had become incapable of implementing methodologies.

Why do I share the story of the teachers who were unable to do inquiry for themselves or transfer those skills to their classrooms? It is because so many of our classically trained educators may actually lack the requisite skills to effectively support the kind of learning you are aiming to offer in your micro-school. Many teachers cognitively know or understand the power of differentiating instruction for every student, but far fewer have seen it in action or truly put it into practice. Some of that is due to the incredible demands on a teacher's time in today's classroom, but more often it's due to the fact that most teachers have never experienced learning that was differentiated for them.

So, what are you to do if you know you need to secure an adult for your micro-school who can facilitate the kinds of innovative learning experiences you envision for your students? As I mentioned earlier, there are a number of colleges and universities that offer an alternative preparation for teaching than the traditional schools of education you can find in most large cities across the globe. You'll need to look more intentionally and ask questions of your applicants to ensure their philosophy of teaching and learning matches yours. And you'll need to be really clear about what kinds of responses you are looking for.

One method you might use is to post your job listing for education staff with the innovative education preparation programs described. You can also utilize the Alternative Education Resource Organization (AERO) in several ways. AERO conducts a once a year conference around the theme of alternative education. You might choose to attend and see what sorts of educators you meet. AERO also offers school builders the ability to advertise their schools and to advertise positions on their website for a fee. Both are great options if you want to get word about your school and staff openings out to a global audience.

Of course, one of your best methods to find teaching staff is to talk about your micro-school to everyone you come in contact with. Posting information in local coffee shops, co-ops, community centers, and so on, is a great way to recruit the sorts of educational staff you are looking for.

Recently, I have begun to facilitate work-related connections between several innovative teacher preparation programs and my school-building clients. If this is something you'd like to know more about, I welcome you to contact me at: mlinaberger@gmail.com.

Finding Your Students and Their Families

One of the most exciting parts of building your micro-school will be finding the families and students whom you will be in service to. Perhaps you already have an amazing circle of friends and family with whom you'll collaborate, which means this chapter will feel old hat to you. If you don't, however, have a handful of kids you know you are going to serve, then this next section will get you thinking about how to find your people.

Finding Your School Community/Tribe

The first – and most logical – place to begin searching for students for your micro-school is in your own backyard. Do you have children living in your neighborhood whom you know and whom you already interact with? Are you a member of the local gym or community center? If so, are there parents you talk with in those locations who have mentioned school issues their children are having?

Another place to not only locate but recruit families for your school is from your client base. If you are a holistic practitioner, like two of my current clients, then you may already be serving parents who have children that could benefit from a school like yours. If this is the case, you can also do intentional gatherings for your clients and their children to talk about the school, making them part of your core team, or part of your decision-making process as you firm up your vision, mission, and special sauce.

Your personal family and friends are another great place to seek out students for your micro-school. These are the people who likely know and love you best. It's quite possible that some of your friends' children are kids who would love to work with you all day as their schooling.

If you are a church goer, this is yet another great place to locate students for your school. Sharing your vision and mission with fellow parishioners, holding informational meetings, or sharing space during the launch of your micro-school are all ways to recruit students as your clients during your start-up phase.

Finally, don't underestimate the power of the internet. If you are considering posting for teachers for your micro-school, you can also advertise for students in similar ways. Social media tools such as Facebook are magnets for parents seeking friendship and wisdom around the parenting of their children. There are various Facebook groups devoted to the topics of homeschooling, unschooling, road-schooling and world-schooling. It's possible that, by joining these groups and talking with parents, you may well find collaborators who are ready to try something different.

I currently maintain a Facebook group devoted to the topic of micro-school building. I welcome you to join us there to talk about your micro-school building project. Search for "micro-school builders" and ask to join. We look forward to meeting you!

Application Process

Once you've figured out where your "tribe" is and where your students may come from, you'll want to consider an application process. Even if you know the kids and families, having them complete an application serves several purposes:

- It creates a mental validation that this is a real school.
- It allows you to clearly state your mission and vision in writing.
- It allows you to communicate any rules, regulations, or stances for learning that are critical to the functioning of your micro-school.
- It allows you to gather information about your prospective students in a private way.
- It allows you to consider your applicants without pressure from them to accept them because of your friendship.
- And, perhaps most importantly, it allows you determine that a student isn't a good fit for your micro-school, and to make recommendations that the stu-

dent attend nearby schools you are in communication with.

It sounds slightly harsh to say – but you may not be able to, nor want to, serve every child who applies to your micro-school. There are any number of reasons you may choose to be more selective about your student population, but the most important is to know your limitations. If you don't know a lot about working with kids who have a particular diagnosis or disability, and you can't hire staff with that expertise, you may want to hold off serving those students until you can secure the appropriate staff to serve the child.

Salary and Benefits

Although these topics appear to be more related to the previous chapter on money, they are here for a reason. Mainly, you will need to consider the value of each of the people you choose to hire to work with you in your micro-school. Some things to ponder are: Will you offer a salary? Will you offer an hourly rate for your employees? Will you offer benefits or retirement contributions? If your staff have students who attend the school, will you offer those children to attend for free or at a reduced cost?

These are all considerations which make working with you more or less attractive to your potential employees. Having a clear idea of how you'll offer remuneration now will help you be clear and concise in your conversation with potential hires.

Chapter 10

Building Block #8 – Ready, Set, GO!

Vision without action is merely a dream.
Action without vision just passes the time.
Vision with action can change the world.

- Joel A. Barker

You've created your vision and mission. You've thought through all of the big components your school will need to make it as a viable alternative for kids today. We need to match your vision to something that helps you create action: actions that you can take, and actions which others can follow as well. You will achieve that through the creation of an actionable business action plan for your micro-school.

One of the very best guides to creating this business plan for your school is to examine the application that is used by states that grant charter school licensure. If you do a search online for "charter school application," you'll come up with both application forms as well as examples of applications that have been completed and approved by various governing bodies. The value in looking at those plans, both varieties, is that you can become familiar with all of the big categories that are commonly defined and described in a school plan.

Some of the key elements that are often included in a charter or private school application for licensure are:

A fact sheet (an abstract or summary of your plan):

This usually includes items such as: the name of your school, its location, facility address, the proposed opening date, leadership team (with contact information), founding families (with contact information)

School Design Components:

- Your mission statement – with philosophy and purpose of school, and mission
- Measurable goals and objectives for learning: both academic and non-academic goals for students
- Educational program: an overview of your chosen "curriculum" and how you'll teach content in all subject areas at various grade levels, how you'll meet individual student needs, what teaching methods you'll use, and a school calendar
- Accountability: how students will be evaluated against your vision and mission statements, how you and your employees will be evaluated, how families and

students will be held accountable for attendance, how you will review budgets and finances, how you will maintain records, how you will share information, how you will enroll students, etc.
- Student evaluation: how you'll measure performance, how you'll measure growth towards objectives, how evaluation will be used to help students improve
- School community: how your school will serve its community, parental and community participation, procedures for reviewing complaints
- Extra-curricular activities: which opportunities you'll offer, how students will engage in other activities, any agreements you've made with other schools or organizations

Needs Assessment:

- Demographics: projected enrollment for the first five years, ultimate enrollment goal, what ages/grades will be served, how many students at each grade/age level, etc.
- Region: where the school will function, why you've chosen the location
- Unique characteristics: describe what makes your school theme or focus different
- Evidence of need: contact with other schools to differentiate yours, how your school will serve students differently than public or private schools, any community support you've received early on

Description of Founding/Management Team:

- Founding group: describe yourself (and partners), including names, background, experience, and references for each (if you have them)

- Discuss how you came together, partnership agreements you have, educational, business, or non-profit partnerships you maintain
- Plans for recruiting other founders/organizers
- Community involvement: describe how you are engaging the community through advertising, media, or meetings
- Governance: how the team and the school will work together
- School calendar (most states, provinces, and countries suggest 990 hours or 180 days of instructional time)
- Staff procedures: appointment, hiring, and firing procedures
- Budget: how it will be adopted, buying/selling of land and buildings, procedures for creating contracts, purchase of materials
- Roles and responsibilities of employees
- School laws and by-laws

Finance and Facility:

- Your preliminary start-up budget
- Fundraising efforts or plans
- Name of business manager/bookkeeper (with contact information)
- Facility: description of the setting and address (with ones being considered listed too)
- Description of facilities' use
- Plan for facilities' maintenance
- Plans to purchase facilities in the future with potential financing options
- Liability and insurance – health, general liability, property, and coverage for the director/employees
- Child accounting: attendance procedures

- Recruiting and marketing plans: how you'll publicize, outreach efforts to families
- Enrollment procedures, student selection, timetables for admitting students, and non-discrimination policies

Implementation and Administration:

- Human resource info: hiring and processes
- Target student/staff ratios
- Training to be offered to staff
- Policies around salary, contracts, hiring, dismissal, sick and other leave, and benefits
- A list of proposed "faculty"
- Keeping of criminal history records for all individuals
- Clearances for staff: child abuse
- Code of conduct for: student behavior, including expulsion, suspension
- Attendance plan and procedures
- Transportation options
- Food service
- Timetable for projected steps, and dates leading to opening
- Safety plans: including building inspection, local fire department inspection
- Other certificates, licenses, etc.
- School health services: illness, administration of medication, etc.

As you can see, most, if not all, of the above items (which came from a charter school application) are things we've talked about in the previous chapters. While we haven't seen them in such a linear form, you are now capable of taking the big headings above, creating a document, and then filling in the information suggested. Doing so will result in the business plan we've been talking about!

Your Accountability Plan

So much more action happens when we have a clear pathway forward. Many business gurus today recommend the use of a 90-day plan of action. This includes key dates and measurable goals, laid out over a 90-day period to guide your work. Without such a plan, it's easy to pick up any task or shiny object that presents itself and to convince yourself that you are actually making progress forward.

In a typical 90-day planning cycle, you will want to think in terms of the following steps:

- define what you expect to happen in the next 12 weeks
- take stock of where you are now
- what has to happen in the next 12 weeks to get you to your goals?
- why do you want to achieve the goals?
- and how will you get to the planned outcome?

The above steps can be broken down further into monthly and weekly processes, to help ensure you stay focused on the bigger vision and mission of your micro-school, while allowing you to accomplish concrete and measurable tasks.

School Year Cycles

The traditional school year, particularly in the United States, has revolved around an agrarian planting schedule. Students typically attended school during the fall, winter, and spring, and were released from studies during the prime growing months to provide support on their family farms. Even though, in most areas, we no longer need to follow an agrarian cycle, many schools still follow the 9-10 months "on" and 2-3 months "off" when it comes to creating school calendars, based mainly on tradition.

As you lay out your business plan, you will want to identify the pattern for school sessions. As was indicated earlier, in many locales, the expectation is for students to attend school 180-190 days per year, for 7-8 hours a day for a total of 990+ hours of "seat time."

It's my recommendation that you continue to adopt that number of days and hours for your micro-school, as it will help to keep you within the state, province, or country guidelines. Where you can innovate, however, is with the months students attend, and the times of day and days of the week when your students attend microschool.

A few innovative public schools have gone to a 4-day school week, with longer hours, to address the rising costs of fuel for busses, and heating and lighting costs. The main challenge with this sort of situation is that it's designed to benefit the school district's need to cut budgets versus the students' needs for extended learning time.

When research showed that middle and high school students performed better when attending school later in the morning, some forward-thinking schools changed start times to benefit student's needs. This is the way in which I encourage you to think about your schedule.

Perhaps you'll run 45-day school cycles with several weeks of vacation in between. Perhaps you'll allow families to gather at the start of the school year to plan out vacations together. Perhaps you'll consider incorporating a whole school travel adventure as part of your school year. Regardless of how you lay out the learning timeframes, it's important to set those out, and commit to them for at least a year before making adjustments.

Mapping Out the School Day

I've had a chance to visit some innovative alternative schools using a wide variety of scheduling strategies to accomplish the tasks related to learning each day. Each has its positives and negatives. I encourage you to visit and talk with as many alternatives as you can to get ideas around how to lay out your learning day.

One of my personal favorites, based on what I have noticed about most kids, is to schedule some dedicated content learning sessions in the morning. Particularly with younger students who are beginning to read, I recommend placing reading time in the morning, to utilize the time of the day when students are most fresh and attentive, to strengthen skills critical to all other types of learning. Subjects such as math, science, and social studies can often be combined into interesting projects. When direct instruction or support is needed in these areas, completing them in the morning often works well too.

Afternoons are a great time for more student freedom and choice. If your students will be doing independent projects, collaborations, or investigations, the afternoon is prime time to allow your students to relax a bit more and to take their time with learning.

Planning for Partnerships

To make your micro-school a rich and powerful learning environment, you'll want to consider working with partners to enhance your students' experiences. As you lay out your business plan, you've likely listed some of your key collaborators. How will you utilize their unique skills and offerings to enhance your students' learning experiences? Now is the time to build those opportunities into your school day, term, or year. Planning ahead for rich partnerships will ensure that you continue to make time for those opportunities to happen.

Planning to Launch

Now that you've worked through the planning process – and have a formal document and set of timelines that articulate what you hope to accomplish with your micro-school – it's time to begin to shop your idea out to key collaborators, parents, and other interested parties. You'll need to craft, at minimum, a six-month plan that includes advertising, meetings for interested parties, and a schedule for setup of the school itself.

Once you've located some key collaborators, you'll likely want to schedule weekly meetings to determine what tasks each person will tend to during the following week. Coming together weekly will ensure that you make progress toward your launch day. As opening day approaches, you'll likely meet more often to tend to the myriad of tasks that unfold.

Now that you have your plan complete and are ready to prepare to launch, you may find that you still have concerns about making your dream a reality. The following chapter on obstacles, pitfalls, and screws-ups holds help to alleviate some of your concerns. If you find after reading them that you still feel you need more help in getting your plans off the ground, I invite you to contact me for a free strategy session. We'll review your plan and determine the best next steps to take. Good luck!

Chapter 11

Obstacles, Pitfalls, and Screw-Ups

Tell me and I'll forget. Show me and I may remember. Involve me and I learn.

- Benjamin Franklin

If you're here with me on this chapter, then you've arrived for one of two reasons. Either you've skipped ahead, based on the title of the chapter, to get an idea about what might go wrong. Or, you've worked your way through the book and have come up with some concerns of your own about how you will get your micro-school up and off the ground.

A lot of obstacles are fabricated in our minds. Many of the pitfalls micro-school builders run into are well-known and avoidable. And the screw-ups many would-be school builders make are actually lessons that can make their work even better.

In many cases, obstacles, pitfalls, and screw-ups are a subtle form of self-sabotage. That's right, you heard me correctly, they aren't so much things that happen to us, but rather things we allow to happen in order to slow our own process. Let me explain.

Almost anything we want to do in this world that's new requires innovation. Our imagination is engaged, we come up with an idea, and we put it to paper. Then we begin to work on the idea and it gains momentum. We continue to work on the idea and refine it. And as time goes on, we may get tired or lose steam. We start to doubt ourselves. And that's when things usually begin to go sideways. When we doubt ourselves, we allow thoughts, like the ones I shared in the first chapter, to slip in. And then we begin to create realities to match the thoughts.

As we discussed earlier – who are you to *not* create this micro-school? In order to help you tackle this task with courage, ease, and grace, let's name any remaining fears or behaviors you might see creep up to derail your plans.

Here are some of the ways I've seen micro-school builders self-sabotage their process:

• *They don't actually DO the process.*

   Reading this book is great, but it won't build a school. In order to build a school, you'll have to do all the steps and put yourself out there to make it happen.

- *They don't create a business/action plan.*

Some micro-school builders get SO excited about their ideas that they go out and start talking about it to everyone who will listen. The problems then crop up when they share different information with different people, leading to differing expectations. It also becomes a problem when they meet up with potential funders. In not seeing a sound action plan, those who could offer up financial support often judge the school builder as a dreamer, not a doer, and they move on to other innovators who do have an action plan.

- *They stick to the comfort of dreaming and wanting to build a school.*

Dreaming is awesome, but it doesn't build schools. Wanting is fine, but it allows personal power to leak out of us slowly. Dreaming and wanting together are rather deadly beyond the initial planning phase, because they lull us into a belief that the time isn't right or that we don't have XYZ to turn things into reality. In truth, there is only the present moment. Waiting for some "perfect time" won't get you there – taking action of any kind, will.

- *They rationalize that their kid will be okay in the current school.*

This is a tough one, and unfortunately, all too common. I'm going to ask you to sit with the statement, "My kid will be okay if I leave him in the school he's in." Can you hear the trouble in the statement? If you are making the statement that he'll be okay – then somewhere deep inside, you know there is something NOT right in the setting and you're making a choice

163

for yourself to do what is most likely easier for YOU, not choosing what's best for your child.

- *They settle for partial success at business and family life.*

This is the one that troubles me the most. If you are the person with a dream to build a school, knowing it will challenge everything, but will pay off in a dream come true for the child and an amazing business for you, then why would you settle for less? This all comes back to the question of: Who are you not to have an amazing business for yourself while also creating an incredible learning setting for your child? If you settle for less than the very best for yourself and your child, then you'll be unknowingly teaching your child to do the very same for himself.

Here are some of the PITFALLS you might encounter (though much less likely now that you're aware of them). YAY!

- *Aiming for less than a legacy.*

I met a woman along my journey named Judy. She and some other parents came up with an idea to create a charter school in their neighborhood. With all her years of experience, Judy knew a ton about how to help kids with a particular type of learning challenge, and so she and her supporters created a school to serve that need. Judy was a veteran teacher, so after a few years of working at the school, she retired for good. A few years later, the principal who had created the school with her retired too.

Within a few years, the school had closed. There was

no one there who could hold the vision. Judy and her collaborators had neglected to aim for leaving a legacy.

- *Not securing expert supporters in their area of weakness.*

This is one of those places where we have to check our egos at the door. If you've done your homework around "people" to serve alongside you, then you'll likely know where you are going to need to secure help. Thinking you can do it all by yourself may well end in disaster.

- *Unclear, incomplete, or confusing business plan (vision, mission, and action steps).*

Writing up a business and action plan to just get the item off of your to-do list won't help you much. Building a clear plan that others can get behind and participate in will. Make sure you build a plan that can actually be understood and implemented by others to ensure that your mission comes to life.

- *A plan that isn't shared or acted upon.*

This sounds strange. Build a plan and then don't follow through. Sadly, it happens more often than you might imagine. To keep yourself from falling into this paralysis trap, be sure to find yourself an accountability partner, someone who believes in you and your mission. Someone who will ask you how it's going and challenge you when you've gotten yourself stalled or stopped.

- *Other things become more important.*

This is perhaps the most deadly pitfall of all. There are spiritual teachings that say, "Energy flows where attention goes." Whatever we focus our attention on is what is most important to us. And it's our attention, energy, and action that make things happen. So if we find ourselves distracted by other things that are "more important," whether they appear to be really urgent or not, then we are taking our attention away from our micro-school building plan.

The last two pitfalls are very real, and very powerful realities that may crop up as you begin to build your micro-school plan. One of the single best ways you can avoid those pitfalls is to work with someone who knows the terrain well and can guide you out of those barren wastelands. If you would like to consider me as your accountability partner or guide, I welcome you to contact me via email at: *mlinaberger@gmail.com* for a complimentary strategy call.

Conclusion

Your School as Your Legacy

Your time is limited, so don't waste it living someone else's life. Don't be trapped by dogma – which is living with the results of other people's thinking. Don't let the noise of others' opinions drown out your own inner voice. And most important, have the courage to follow your heart and intuition.

- Steve Jobs

As you have seen, micro-school building is a real and viable alternative to school as it is. Micro-schools are also a wonderful way for those with an entrepreneurial spirit to offer their children an amazing learning environment while also creating a viable business for themselves.

Over the course of this book we've talked about the eight foundational blocks you'll need to lay as part of the micro-school building process. To review, they were:

Building Block #1 - Frame your WHY with a PLAN
Building Block #2 - Get Legalities Out of the Way!
Building Block #3 - What's YOUR Special Sauce?
Building Block #4 - Location, Location, Location
Building Block #5 - Show Me the Money!
Building Block #6 - David vs. Goliath
Building Block #7 - People, People, People
Building Block #8 - Ready, Set, GO!

Now that you've reached the end, and you've crafted your business and action plans, it's time to bring your vision to life. My wish for you:

- May you find your reason WHY, the perfect purpose for building YOUR micro-school.
- May you skillfully craft your micro-school to launch and grow within the legalities in which you operate.
- May your particular micro-school "flavor" excite and inspire children to reach their highest potential.
- May your location feel warm and inviting to all who enter the space.
- May the financial resources you need to open and operate find their way to you quickly and with ease.
- May the learning pathways you choose for children inspire them to go above and beyond what is currently being taught in most schools.
- May you identify and employ the most talented and compassionate individuals in your school.
- And may you walk forward with your plans boldly, creating a micro-school that does far more than you ever imagined.

And finally, I wish that your school may become a legacy that you, your collaborators, and the families you serve may be proud of. May it be a lasting testament to your vision for the children of today and tomorrow. May children look back in hundreds of years, thinking fondly of you and the sacrifices you made for them, in order to leave an amazing legacy for them!

I'd love to hear about your ideas and to know how the book has helped you to bring your vision to life. If you're willing to share your story with me, please reach out at: mlinaberger@gmail.com and tell me more about your story.

As a special think you for taking this journey with me, I'd love to send you a copy of my first book, *HELP! My Child Hates School: An Awakened Parent's Guide to Action*. If you email me and say "First book please," I'll send out a digital copy to you right away.

I also invite you to keep an eye out for some special offers I make from time to time to help you directly with the micro-school building process. You can find out more about those on my website at: www.maralinaberger.com.

Acknowledgments

Writing a second book felt much easier than the first. With all the preliminary thank-you's covered there, I want to acknowledge the people who've been most present and supportive during the past year as I wrote this second book.

Thanks to Angela, for helping me to launch the first book in style. For coaching me through all the tough moments when I wanted to hide and shrink from defining my mission and bringing it to life. For providing me chances to shine on bigger stages. For putting my book in the hands of key influencers and singing my praises to those who need to hear. And most of all, for trusting her son's education to the processes covered in both of my books.

Thanks to Sir Edward, Lady Sophia, Sir Doc, Princess Michaela, and all the Angel Knights. It has been a joy to join your company, to dedicate myself further to your mission of empowering children all over the globe. I'm grateful to have the chance to serve by your side, and to help birth your new Legacy School!

Thanks to all of the fellow authors who have shared time and space with me. Listening to ideas, talking me through challenges, and allowing me to support them in return. The friendships and connections we've made while working side-by-side to build our businesses have been priceless. I count them amongst my closest of friends.

To my biological family – Dad, Sandi, Anne, Tom, Betsy, Brian, JT, and Liam – thanks for continuing to encourage me as I build my business into something I can truly be proud of.

To Sarah and Sami, and their awesome husbands, Steve and Rob. Thanks for inviting me into your lives and making me feel truly welcome.

And to Michael, the new partner who encouraged me with an open heart and open arms as I was contemplating this second book. You've taught me so much about resiliency, about how our brains work differently, and about how we can meet each other eye to eye through love. I am thrilled to share my life with you, to have your keen eyes and ears watching over my progress as I grow my business. And I am beyond grateful you've drawn me into the world of ballroom dancing – I can't imagine any better way to spend an evening!

About the Author

Mara Linaberger's essential belief is that each of us has chosen to be here on the planet at this moment in time for a specific reason – that we're all on a mission we chose for ourselves. And that figuring out what it is that we love, what we're good at, and why we've chosen to be here now, is the main reason for continuing to engage in rich and meaningful learning throughout a lifetime. Mara also believes that many schools actually slow down or stifle those goals and outcomes. So she's passionate about helping parents create micro-schools that put education to work, serving kids as they develop their highest potentials while also having fun learning!

Mara is a life-long educator, author, musician, and artist, having spent 25 years in service as a public school educator, teacher trainer, and administrator. First earning her doctorate in Instructional Technology, Mara then went on to earn a Superintendent's Letter of Eligibility in the state of Pennsylvania. Having seen the reality of school from top to bottom, she changed directions. Launching "Mindful Technology Consultants" in 2013, she has provided individualized training and support services for online coaches, small businesses, school districts, and larger organizations. Focused on the simplified and intentional use of technology, she helps clients to deconstruct complex language and ideas in order to achieve harmony, to make rich connections between like-minded creative folks, and to bring back a love for creativity and learning.

Mara currently lives with her partner Michael "in Harmony" - just outside of Pittsburgh, PA, while she travels far and wide, directly supporting teachers and parents who are interested in building a micro-school, to implement their business plan quickly, effectively and efficiently.

About the Cover

When I wrote my first book, HELP! My Child Hates School: An Awakened Parent's Guide to Action, I was surprised by the cover options the designer offered. The cover that I ultimately chose, featured a young girl in a super hero costume, complete with red cape and boxing gloves. I loved the photo because of the message of power and creativity it conveyed. It suggested that our children are super heroes in disguise, ready for a challenge!

As I began working with the Good Knight Child Empowerment Network in Maryland on their micro-school plan, I had a chance to become acquainted with many of the print materials they had created over the years. One of the classic photos used over and over was an image of the founder, Sir Edward dressed as the blue knight, micro-school builder Lady Sophia dressed as Snow White, and her daughter, then a toddler, Michaela dressed as Super Girl. Michaela's little image reminded me so much of the girl on my book cover, I jokingly told her that the cover photo WAS her!

As I was working on the micro-school building book, I had brainstorming conversations with both Michaela and Jesse, who hopes to attend the Legacy School someday When Jesse noticed the connection between he first cover and Michaela, he said to me, "I want to be on the cover of your second book!"

The cover you'll find on this book was the brainchild of Jesse. He thought an image of he and Michaela "building a school" would send the right kind of message to prospective readers. On the day of the photo shoot, we looked for spots on the Good Knight Castle property which would showcase the two kids engaged in the act of building. The final photo chosen features Jesse and Michaela working on a small playhouse like building in front of a castle wall. Both the wall and the playhouse had been created by Sir Edward and his many volunteer knights as part of the castle's museum displays.

At nearly thirty years old, many of the displays are in need of restoration. Michaela, Jesse, and their classmates at the Legacy School, will have an opportunity to document the work of Sir Edward and his colleagues and to determine the next steps in restoring and upgrading various buildings on the property. Truly an opportunity to add to the Legacy of the organization.

I hope that the picture of the two children working together to expand on what has been achieved in the past inspires you to include children in your own microschool planning process!

Thank You!

If you've read this far, THANK YOU. I know everyone doesn't read books from front to back anymore! So if you've stuck in it with me, I have a couple of gifts to offer as a thank you!

I'd love to offer you a free copy of my first book, *HELP! My Child Hates School: An Awakened Parent's Guide to Action.* Please visit my website: www.maralinaberger.com for the free download.

How do you know for sure that opening a micro-school for your child is the best course of action for YOU? If you still have any nagging doubts, I've created a quiz to help you assess where you are and recommend the best course of action for you and your child. Shoot me an email at mlinaberger@gmail.com with the words "quiz please" in the subject line, and I'll get it right out to you.

Would you like to talk about your micro-school idea and get my professional support or input? Would you like to explore whether or not we're a good fit to work together? Then please contact me to set up a free 30-minute consultation to get clarity around your ideas.